Knowing Christ

Knowing Christ

S. Craig Glickman

MOODY PRESS

CHICAGO

ISBN: 0-8024-3502-5

Printed in the United States of America

I gratefully dedicate this book to:

Zane Hodges and S. Lewis Johnson,
   who taught me to interpret the New Testament;
Bill Starr and Roy McKasson,
   who first awakened in me a deep love for Christ;
my students at Dallas Seminary,
   for whom these studies were first begun;
and Dr. Charles Ryrie,
   whose encouragement brought
      this work to completion.

CONTENTS

Foreword 7

1. Mirror, Mystery, and Miracle 9

2. The Waters of Judgment 17

3. The Wilderness of Conflict 35

4. The Mountain of Splendor 61

5. The Hill of Sacrifice .89

6. The Plain of Battle 131

7. Patterns, Pride, and Promises 171

FOREWORD

Seldom have I read a book that so stimulated my mind and refreshed my heart as this one did. Combining good theology, careful exegesis, and beautiful syntheses of biblical passages, Mr. Glickman has woven a unique tapestry of the life and ministry of the Lord Jesus found nowhere else that I know of.

Even familiar passages like those concerning the baptism and temptation of Christ shine with new facets of insights the author gives to them. Old Testament passages which foreshadow or parallel the events of our Lord's life come alive in a fresh way. The ultimate future triumph of the King is described in an unforgettable manner.

Reading this book could be for any reader a significant spiritual experience, helping to conform him to the image of the One about whom it is so well written.

CHARLES C. RYRIE

1

MIRROR, MYSTERY, AND MIRACLE

For this is the marriage of heaven and earth:
Perfect myth and perfect fact:
Claiming not only our love and our obedience,
    but also our wonder and delight.

C. S. Lewis

What is the most important thing to do in life? If a person could accomplish only one goal, what should it be? A wise man once asked Christ that question, and He returned a swift and sure answer. He said that the greatest commandment is: "YOU SHALL LOVE THE LORD YOUR GOD WITH ALL YOUR HEART, AND WITH ALL YOUR SOUL, AND WITH ALL YOUR MIND, AND WITH ALL YOUR STRENGTH" (Mark 12:30).

It is doubtful if anyone will ever understand completely what this duty involves. But one can be certain that it necessitates at least two things. First, that God be known. For one cannot love someone he does not know. And second, that God be followed. For one cannot love someone he is not willing to follow.

A Christian realizes that so lofty a goal as loving God can be accomplished only through Christ. For through Christ, God is both known and followed.

Through Christ, God is known because Christ is the visible image of the invisible God (Col. 1:15; John 1:1, 14, 18). He is the eternal God who took upon Himself flesh and blood—not only to accomplish the most important mission of all time, but also to reveal to us the Father (John 1:18; Phil. 2:5-11; Heb. 1:1-3; 2:14). Thus the Lord Jesus could truly say, "He who has seen Me has seen the Father" (John 14:9), and the apostle John could affirm that "Whoever denies the Son does not have the Father; the one who confesses the Son has the Father also" (1 John 2:23). So through Christ, God is known.

But also through Christ, God is followed. For Christ, through the Spirit, transforms a Christian and enables that one to follow Him. So through Christ, God is loved because through Christ, God is known and followed.

The apostle Paul affirmed this in an unforgettable way in his second letter to the Corinthian Christians. For in a portion of that letter he described Christ as the One beheld in a miraculous mirror, who reflects the invisible God and, through the Spirit, transforms those who behold Him (2 Cor. 3:18). The context of this passage unfolds the fulness of its meaning.

> But thanks be to God, who always leads us in His triumph in Christ, and manifests through us the sweet aroma of the knowledge of Him in every place. [15]For we are a fragrance of Christ to God among those who are being saved and among those who are perishing; [16]to the one an aroma from death to death, to the other an aroma from life to life. And who is adequate for these things? [17]For we are not like many, peddling the word of God, but as from sincerity, but as from God, we speak in Christ in the sight of God.
>
> Are we beginning to commend ourselves again? Or do we need, as some, letters of commendation to you or from you? [2]You are our letter, written in our hearts, known and read by all men; [3]being manifested that you are a letter of Christ, cared for by us, written not with ink, but with the Spirit of the living God, not on tablets of stone, but on tablets of human hearts. [4]And such confidence we have through Christ toward God. [5]Not that we are adequate in ourselves to consider anything as coming from ourselves, but our adequacy is from God, [6]who also made us adequate as servants of a

new covenant, not of the letter, but of the Spirit; for the letter kills, but the Spirit gives life. [7]But if the ministry of death, in letters engraved on stones, came with glory, so that the sons of Israel could not look intently at the face of Moses because of the glory of his face, fading as it was, [8]how shall the ministry of the Spirit fail to be even more with glory? [9]For if the ministry of condemnation has glory, much more does the ministry of righteousness abound in glory. [10]For indeed what had glory, in this case has no glory on account of the glory that surpasses it. [11]For if that which fades away was with glory, much more that which remains is in glory.

[12]Having therefore such a hope, we use great boldness in our speech, [13]and are not as Moses, who used to put a veil over his face that the sons of Israel might not look intently at the end of what was fading away. [14]But their minds were hardened; for until this very day at the reading of the old covenant the same veil remains unlifted, because it is removed in Christ. [15]But to this day whenever Moses is read, a veil lies over their heart; [16]BUT WHENEVER A MAN TURNS TO THE LORD, THE VEIL IS TAKEN AWAY. [17]Now the Lord is the Spirit; and where the Spirit of the Lord is, there is liberty. [18]But we all, with unveiled face beholding as in a mirror the glory of the Lord, are being transformed into the same image from glory to glory, just as from the Lord, the Spirit (2 Cor. 2:14—3:18).

Paul had begun to explain to his readers the unequalled importance of his message about Christ (2 Cor. 2:14-17). It was a matter of eternal life and eternal death for everyone who heard it (2 Cor. 2:15-16). Therefore, he faithfully proclaimed the message without compromise (2 Cor. 2:17).

Realizing that some might accuse him of bragging, Paul asked his Corinthian friends if they thought that he was commending himself or needed their recommendation to qualify him for so important a task (2 Cor. 3:1). He answered his own question very simply. Neither they nor he could so commend him that he would be qualified to proclaim so important a message.

But God could and did qualify Paul to speak with such confidence (2 Cor. 2:17; 3:4-5, 12, 17; 4:1). And the life-transforming work of God's Spirit in the Corinthians' lives confirmed this (2 Cor. 3:2-18). For through Christ, the Spirit of God transformed the lives of those who beheld God the Father in the miraculous mirror in which the Son is seen.

To this mirror, Paul referred by saying, "But we all, with unveiled face beholding as in a mirror the glory of the Lord, are being transformed into the same image from glory to glory, just as from the Lord, the Spirit" (2 Cor. 3:18).[1]

Christ, of course, is both the mirror and the image seen in it, for when the eternal Son took upon Himself flesh and blood, He became a mirror in which we saw the character of God. His incarnation produced the mirror, and His life gave us the image.

And the miraculous nature of the mirror shows why Christ is the One through whom God is loved. It is miraculous, first of all, because it reflects not the visible but the invisible. We see not our visible selves but the invisible God. For Christ is the visible image of the invisible God. And second, it is miraculous because it transforms us who gaze into the mirror into the image of the One we see. We become what we see in the mirror, and thus transformed, follow Christ and love the Father.

But this is not merely desirable; it is absolutely necessary. For as we stand before His genuine goodness, we learn of our true sinfulness.

THE TRANSFORMATION PROCESS

Therefore, the first look in the mirror, Paul affirmed, must be a special one that brings forgiveness and life. We must turn from gazing only at rules of life and look at the Giver of life (2 Cor. 3:4-11). Until then, the rules serve primarily to condemn us because we cannot keep them. However, when we look at Christ in order to see God, the Spirit takes the veil of blindness from our eyes; we accept the forgiveness and life that He offers, and the rules of God's way of life become mysteriously written on our hearts. Then from deep within us, we desire to keep God's rules and to serve Him (2 Cor. 3:2-3, 16). But the initial look must begin the transformation.

Keeping our eyes on Him will continue it. This is not simply looking at a literal picture, of course. This is looking at Christ, as a woman may look continuously at her much-loved husband. And as she grows in her knowledge of him, so she grows in her love for him. Similarly, as we grow in our knowledge of Christ, so will we grow in our love for Him. And then, by the mysterious working of the Spirit of God, we will become progressively like Christ—"from glory to glory," Paul said—from one degree of glorious change to the next.

SWANS AND UGLY DUCKLINGS

The transformation is not without its ups and downs, we must admit. Perhaps many of us in the process shall, in fact, repeat the story of the Ugly Duckling. In the beginning, he had a very unfortunate time. He was more awkward and less attractive than the ducks he grew up beside, and they ridiculed his differences. Fleeing their abuse, he took shelter in a home whose pets were a chicken and a cat. He was rejected here, too, because he could not lay eggs like a hen or purr like a kitten. "You just do not understand me," he told them, but he was treated only with scorn.

Then one day he beheld the graceful and elegant swans, the most beautiful birds he had ever seen. A strange feeling came over him. "He turned somersaults in the water, stretched his neck trying to follow their flight, and uttered a cry so loud that it quite frightened him. . . . When he finally lost sight of them, he dived right down to the very bottom of the water, and when he came up, he was quite beside himself. He had no idea what the birds were called or where they were going; he only knew that he loved them as he had never loved anything before."[2]

Another winter came with all its struggles. But, at last, spring melted the ice of the ponds. And as the Ugly Duckling was swimming, he saw again two of those beautiful birds. Soon they swam towards him. The closer they came, the more frightened he became. Then when such beauty was right in front of him, he bowed his head in humility and covered his face with his wing.

However, when he bowed his head, he saw his reflection in the water for the very first time. And in speechless amazement, he saw that he too was a swan. Slowly uncovering his wing from his face, he lifted his head from the pond. He did not raise it proudly and high, as an ostrich would, but humbly as a swan, slightly bent over in an expression of gratitude. Then he swam off with his fellow swans.

Perhaps our own experiences are similar to his. Our first look to Christ in faith may often be like the Ugly Duckling's first look at the swans—accompanied more by excitement than understanding. We, of course, know why the Ugly Duckling was so beside himself when he first saw the swans. He responded from his innermost being, because he was made to be a swan, too. But at that moment he did not understand all this.

Similarly, we may respond to Christ from so deep within ourselves that we cannot explain every reason for our belief. Nevertheless, we do respond, because God has created us to be like the Great One we see in the miraculous mirror. Then we, like the Ugly Duckling, learn more of ourselves and more of the One we love, after we have already responded.

As we continue to behold Christ, the image of God, the transformation in our lives will be as lovely as that of the Ugly Duckling who became a swan. We, like the swan, will become what we were born to be. Then with humility in our walk and gratitude in our hearts, we will live our lives before God; then we may love the Lord our God with all our hearts, souls, minds, and strength. That is how we may fulfill the greatest commandment, the most important goal of life.

But, of course, this all presupposes we learn more of God's Son, the Lord Jesus Christ. And that is what the rest of this book is about, learning more of the Son, the miraculous mirror who transforms our lives. In five crucial episodes of His life, we shall see His character unfold.

2

THE WATERS OF JUDGMENT

Who is this hero, then, does he say?
Where does he come from? What has he with him?
Does he come armed with weapons of war?
Has he a great following behind him?
Or alone . . . goes he as a merchant
   who travels into alien lands?[1]
>   Bacchylides of Ceos, fifth century B.C.,
>   *The Coming of Theseus*

Among the rivers of the earth, the River Jordan had no equals. Geographers knew her as the lowest river on the planet. Historians acknowledged her banks as the home of some of civilization's earliest settlers. Students of religion recognized her as the central river in a land where three world religions had originated—Judaism, Islam, and Christianity.

She recorded the history of Israel in her waters. Across her waters Joshua had led the people into the promised land. Beside her waters the great prophets Elijah and Elisha had parted. In her waters Naaman the leper had been healed. Through her waters King David had fled the conspiracy of Absalom.

She had witnessed the deeds of some of history's most illustrious men. And for that she is rightly honored. But she received her highest honor when the Nazarene came to her banks. Before Him, the others should all bow—historians, geographers, students, Joshua, prophets, and kings. He had not come to be worshiped, however. He had come because it was His time of choice.

Until now, He had lived in the soft coolness of Nazareth, where the rolling hills of Galilee surrounded Him with luxurious fields and orchards. The flowers, fields, and fruit trees clothed the countryside with rich browns, greens, and colorful pastels. And how lovely they were now in the fall.

But this was the fall of A.D. 30, and He must leave Galilee. The time had come for His journey to the River Jordan. To reach His destination, He must descend the hills of Galilee, cross the lowlands of the valley, then travel through the desert called the wilderness of Judea.

He had not traveled far from Nazareth before He saw what daily temperatures of over 100 degrees could do to a land without water. Autumn rains may possibly have come, but the effects of the scorching summer sun remained. Soon He was surrounded by the dry, barren wasteland. In every direction was nothing but the silent, suffocating sand. Its hot surface yielded only wave after wave of heat. The waves rolled upward, blurred the horizon, and seemed to melt every object into strange, liquid forms. No doubt Jesus shook His head and squinted His eyes to see more clearly. The desert only whisked its sand in the distance, sometimes over His path, even across His sweat-streaked face.

But on He walked to the Jordan. At last the thick, tangled foliage along its banks appeared as a dark line on the horizon. Almost at the same time, a group of people emerged like dots beside it. As He came closer, He saw they were gathered around a tall, rugged man standing in the Jordan. Occasionally, members of the crowd entered the water to be baptized by him. Finally, Jesus could understand his words and see him clearly.

But He recognized the man before He heard his words or saw his face. For He and all Israel knew that John the Baptist was proclaiming a baptism of repentance for the forgiveness of sin. God Himself, through the ancient prophets, had foretold this work of John that Jesus now saw. "As it is written in Isaiah the prophet, 'BEHOLD, I SEND MY MESSENGER BEFORE YOUR FACE, WHO WILL PREPARE YOUR WAY; THE VOICE OF ONE CRYING IN THE WILDERNESS, "MAKE READY THE WAY OF THE LORD, MAKE HIS PATHS STRAIGHT" ' " (Mark 1:2-3). John's proclamation was intended to prepare a righteous people for a righteous king.

But this was not the first time a people were prepared in the wilderness to serve God. Centuries before, God had brought the nation out of Egypt, across the Red Sea, into the wilderness, and, at last, to the promised land. These events marked the official creation of Israel. In fact, Moses declared that God had given the nation birth when He had brought them through the Sea to the wilderness (Deut. 31:30; 32:10-18). There He taught them to obey Him, to walk like a son before his father (Hos. 11:1-3). And furthermore, as a husband and wife enter into a binding relationship specified in the marriage agreement; so in the wilderness, after the Red Sea, God entered into a binding relationship with the newborn nation, specified in an agreement called the covenant of Moses. It was so called because God made the agreement through Moses as a representative for the entire nation.

But the time had come for a new birth of the nation and a new agreement, called the new covenant. Prophets, in previous eras, had frequently entreated the people of Israel to return to God and to the old covenant of Moses. Then for 400 years before John, the voice of the prophets had been silent. But now the prophet John was crying out for the people to return to God again—in the last days of the old covenant, but in preparation for a new covenant.

How appropriate, indeed, how symbolic it was for the nation to return to God in the wilderness. There God had given them birth in the past. Now if they would return to Him there, He would give the nation new birth in the present under a righteous King to come. As they had passed through the Red Sea to sonship in a wilderness once before, so now they could pass through the waters of the Jordan to renew their sonship in a wilderness again.

Some had come to do so. And Jesus had come with them. But He had not come as an observer. He had come to this place to choose the path of duty like a Hercules. And as Theseus came to move the stone and take his sword and sandals, so our Lord had come to set the course of His life, too. The following words etched this event on the pages of history.

"Then Jesus arrived from Galilee at the Jordan coming to John, to be baptized by him. But John tried to prevent Him, saying, 'I have need to be baptized by You, and do You come to me?' But Jesus answering said to him, 'Permit it at this time; for in this way it is fitting for us to fulfill all righteousness.' Then he permitted Him. And after being baptized, Jesus went up immediately from the water; and behold, the heavens were opened, and he saw the Spirit of God descending as a dove, and coming upon Him, and behold, a voice out of the heavens, saying, 'This is My [Son, the Beloved] in whom I am well-pleased' "[2] (Matt. 3:13-17).

A STRANGE BEGINNING

As John had been baptizing others, he had been saying, "After me comes One who is mightier than I, and I am not even fit to stoop down and untie the thong of His sandals.

I baptized you with water; but He will baptize you with the Holy Spirit" (Mark 1:7-8).

No wonder John was puzzled that the One whose sandals he was "not even fit to remove" (Matt. 3:11) should condescend to be baptized by him. And John would not be the only one to question why Jesus would undergo the baptism of repentance. It seemed a contradiction in terms, at least a contradiction with other Scriptures. For throughout their pages, His sinlessness was claimed a necessity for His task and a credential for His acceptance. It was paraded before His followers (Isa. 53:9; 2 Cor. 5:21; 1 Pet. 2:22). And He Himself honestly affirmed it (John 8:46). But if He were not being baptized for His sins, why was He being baptized at all?

Look again at His reason. He said it was "to fulfill all righteousness." In some way, this was a necessary act of obedience to His Father's will. But in what particular way was it necessary? How does this fulfill God's requirements for His life?

BURDENS BY BIRTH

I think this is the explanation. When He was born a citizen of Israel, He accepted all the responsibilities of that citizenship. He observed its laws and ceremonies. He even submitted to the consequences of Israel's sin. It is easy to overlook this. But, for example, as a citizen of Israel, Jesus was under the rule of Rome. And yet the forfeiting of self-rule by the nation was a direct result of her disobedience to God in the past. So in a very real way, Jesus had accepted the consequence of Israel's sin in yielding to the rule of Rome.

Now the nation was being called to repentance in the wilderness because of her sin. And though some members of the nation may have been more responsible than other members, the entire nation was considered guilty.

For example, a few military leaders in Russia might be mainly responsible for launching an attack on the United States, but the consequences of American retaliation would affect even the Russian factory workers who merely supported the economy. As a nation, they would be guilty. And so it was with Israel and her people.

Thus, as a citizen of Israel, called by Israel's prophet to repentance for the nation's sin, Jesus came to the wilderness. He came in repentance not for His sin, but for the nation's. As He had taken the consequences of their sin upon Himself in submitting to Roman rule, so He now took the consequences of their sin in heeding the call to national repentance.

It may seem strange to us that One without sin would repent, in effect, for the sins of others. But it was not so unusual to the nation of Israel. In the past, a number of its leaders had foreshadowed such identification, not in being sinless, but at least in repenting for national sins not specifically their own.

Long ago, the prophet Daniel had been taken into captivity, not for his sins but for the sins of his nation. Yet because he was a member of that nation, the consequences of those sins were his in a very real sense. He, therefore, prayed, "Open shame belongs to *us*, O Lord, to our kings, our princes, and our fathers, because *we* have sinned against Thee" (Dan. 9:8, itals. added).

Ezra, too, a leader after the time of Daniel, embraced a similar experience. Although he had not been unfaithful to God, upon hearing of the unfaithfulness of other Israelites, he prayed for the forgiveness of all the nation: "O my God, I am ashamed and embarrassed to lift up my face to Thee, my God, for *our* iniquities have risen above our heads, and *our* guilt has grown even to the heavens" (Ezra 9:6, itals. added).

The righteous leaders of the past had, in humility, accepted the consequences of the sins of their fellow citizens. In surpassing humility, the sinless Nazarene now accepted them, too. And in so doing, He foreshadowed the ultimate purpose of His mission: To accept the consequences of others' sins in a way that no ordinary man could possibly do.

A Purpose Foreshadowed

Baptism was a particularly effective way to foreshadow this work—not merely because it was a sign of repentance, but also because it was a symbolic picture of His death and resurrection (Mark 10:38; Rom. 6:4). In His death, He was submerged under the waters of judgment meant for others, but He emerged from them in resurrection life.

Yet not only did His baptism look forward to His ultimate purpose, but it also looked back to the ancient origins of that purpose, when leaders of God's people led their followers through the waters of judgment. It looked back first to the Red Sea.

The Red Sea and the Great Flood

There Moses miraculously had led his people through its waters, but the Egyptians had perished in the same waters. Because this event pictured baptism, and, consequently, the work of Christ, Paul in the New Testament could say that those who believed Moses were "baptized into him" (1 Cor. 10:2). This means they believed him, allied themselves to him, and so identified with him that his fate became theirs. Thus they who belonged to Moses passed through the Red Sea; they who belonged to Pharaoh drowned. Similarly, they who belong to Christ will pass through the judgment on sin to life. They who belong elsewhere will not. So the origin of God's purpose to deliver through the waters of judgment goes back at least thirty-four centuries to Moses.

But if we squint our eyes a bit, we may see back even further. Several centuries before Moses, Noah had also been instrumental in leading others through the waters of judgment. They who believed him about the future, who identified with him so that his experience became theirs, passed through the flood waters of judgment to life on land again. The apostle Peter saw in this event a picture of our identification with Christ by faith, in whom we pass through the judgment waters of sin to life (1 Pet. 3:19-21). So the origin of God's purpose to deliver through waters of judgment goes back not only to Moses, but even to Noah.

Perhaps, however, it goes back even further, not to an earlier man, but to a time when no man existed at all; a time when there was only darkness, silence, emptiness, and universal sea. That is the description of planet Earth in the beginning (Gen. 1:2).

WATERS OF THE FIRST SEA

Some believe that this is a description of the first stage of creation, and that from this raw material, God created the universe. Others believe that it was the result of a judgment on the earth, which occurred before the creative acts of Genesis 1. Still others believe that it was simply a chaotic state, the origin of which we know nothing except that God was not its author. Everyone agrees, however, that this dark, empty, chaotic scene was a desolate place insufficient for life.

Perhaps that is why this description of darkness, chaos, emptiness, and universal sea became customary images in the Old Testament for sin and death. For sin also brings these four things. It causes a terrifying darkness, in which a person further loses his way and stumbles, as he blindly gropes through life. It results in a confusing chaos and disorder in his life purpose and direction. It leaves one with agonizing emptiness and loneliness. And, finally, ᴀ creates the frustration and restlessness pictured in the tossing and turning of the sea.

Perhaps we are not surprised by the first three images but question the fourth. That is understandable, for it is not as well known that the sea was frequently referred to as a picture of sin's consequences. Nevertheless, a careful study of its use in the Scripture will reveal this.[3] Hence in the new heaven and new earth of God's perfect kingdom, not only will there be no darkness, chaos, or emptiness, but no sea as well! (Rev. 21:1, 4; 22:3-5) Nevertheless, in the beginning, all was covered by sea (Gen. 1:2).

Into this dreadful primeval world, the God of heaven came. Where there was darkness, He made light. Where there was chaos, He brought order. Where there was emptiness, He brought life. And where there was only the never-ending waters of the sea—the waters of judgment, for no man could live there—God brought dry land. He brought the dry land out from the waters of judgment to establish a stable place for man to live.

Does this not portray the meaning of Christ's baptism? For He, too, came out of the waters of judgment to stable land—in truth, to be the stable land Himself—not only after the Jordan, but after the waters of judgment at the cross. For there, in resurrection, He established a stable place for man to live; a rock of salvation, Scripture says, which one stands upon by faith in Him.

So first, God Himself brought the foundation for life through the waters of judgment in creation. Next, He used Noah and Moses to lead people through twice more. Then, at last, neither God alone, nor God through man, but God as man, the Son of God, came to be Himself the land of life brought through the waters of judgment. That was His mission, and its origin went back to the beginning of time.

25

nified not only His purpose and its origin,
ficial acceptance of His task. The great
prophets, priests, and kings of Israel were usually inaugurated to their tasks by the anointing of oil. In this way,
they expressed their need and received God's provision of
His Holy Spirit to accomplish their work. Yet because the
work of Jesus was so colossal in comparison to any done
before, not a symbol of the Spirit, but the Spirit Himself,
in the form of a dove, descended upon Him.

The Spirit of God had hovered like a dove over the first
creation in the beginning (Gen. 1:2). There He had
brought the dry land from the sea. Now He came upon the
Son of God, to empower Him to create a new land of
safety for everyone who became part of the new creation
through faith in Him (Rom. 8:18-22; 2 Cor. 5:17; 2 Pet.
3:13). That is why the anointing of Jesus was by the Holy
Spirit Himself.

THUNDER AND LIGHTNING

It was customary, upon the anointing of a man for office,
to proclaim the official title of the one anointed. A
prophet, for example, would anoint a man to be king and
proclaim him such at the same time (1 Sam. 10:1; 2 Kings
9:6). But as the Holy Spirit, rather than oil, came upon
Christ, so God the Father, rather than any man, proclaimed His official title.

"This is My [Son, the Beloved] in whom I am well-
pleased." His voice thundered the words, and their meaning electrified the sky of the first century.

They may appear to be ordinary words to us, but, of
course, some very significant words to us of the twentieth
century might seem ordinary to people of the first century, too. For example, if an official, counting presidential
election returns, emerged from his office and said to a

candidate, "Hail to the Chief," the words would mean more than "hello." He would have, by his greeting, just announced the next president of the United States. And we would be aware of his meaning, because the phrase "Hail to the Chief" is a greeting reserved for that office. I suppose every nation has similar phrases with special meaning to them.

The nation of Israel certainly had its share of significant phrases. And when the Father spoke at the baptism, He weaved together no less than three of these to form an astonishing proclamation of the identity of Jesus.

DISCOVERY

The first phrase, "This is My [Son]," is a fascinating one, but it contains a preliminary puzzle. It is this: Mark and Luke record the Father as saying not "This is My [Son]," but "Thou art My . . . Son" (Mark 1:11; Luke 3:22). It may be a small difference, but it deserves attention.

At least three explanations are possible. Two stem from a closer look at the phrase, "Thou art My . . . Son." It is a direct quotation of Psalm 2:7, and, therefore, would immediately direct a reader to its original meaning in that passage. So one explanation might be that the literal words of the Father were, "This is My [Son]," but Mark and Luke knew that the precise meaning of the literal words was derived from Psalm 2:7. Therefore, not wanting people to miss that original meaning, they directed their readers' attention unmistakably to it. For example, if the official, counting election returns, said, "Hail to the Chief," most Americans would know his meaning. But a foreign translator might report, "The official emerged from his office and said, 'You are the next president.' " Similarly, perhaps Matthew gave the literal words, and Mark and Luke gave the literal meaning.

Another very possible explanation is simply this: God

said both. To the audience around His Son, He said, "This is My [Son],"; then directly to Jesus, He said, "Thou art My . . . Son." Then, as frequently happened, the gospel writers selectively recorded the words deemed most significant to them.

Finally, it is commonly suggested that "This is My [Son]" is simply an *indirect* quotation, whereas "Thou art My . . . Son" is a *direct* quotation. This is a perfectly adequate explanation, and surely we must grant the gospel writers the freedom to use either a direct or indirect quotation.

SONSHIP AND KINGSHIP

At any rate, this much is clear: The meaning of the first phrase of the Father's proclamation will be found in Psalm 2. The psalm begins by describing a conspiracy that had formed against the Lord and His anointed King (Psalm 2:1-3). That King was secure, however, for the Lord reaffirmed His installation of Him as King of Israel (vv. 4-6). Then the King Himself spoke of that very installation, when He said, "I will surely tell of the [Lord's legal statute]:[4] He said to Me, 'Thou art My Son, today I have begotten Thee' " (v. 7).

What did the Lord mean in saying, upon the inauguration of the King, "Thou art My Son, today I have begotten Thee"? In what legal statute do we discover the sense in which He became God's Son? Hebrews 1:5 tells us the legal statute establishing His reign and sonship is recorded in 2 Samuel 7:12-16.

The statute is contained in a broader legal agreement made with King David, wherein he was promised a royal line of descent. And every king who descended from him, upon assuming his kingship, would, at the same time, enter into a Father-son relationship with God (2 Sam. 7:14; Psalm 89:26). Therefore, in a sense, the prince became God's son when he was inaugurated as king. Thus the Lord could quite naturally say, "Thou art My Son, today I have begotten Thee" (Psalm 2:7). The prince at that moment entered the father-son relationship, promised every king descended from David. That moment, figuratively speaking, he was given birth as God's son. And so it was with Christ at His baptism.

Does this mean that Jesus was not the Son of God before His baptism? No, not at all. It only means He was not a Son in this sense of the word until then. He was the eternal Son, even before His birth (John 1:1, 14; 5:18). But not until He became a man, was He a Son by birth (Luke 1:35). And not until His baptism and anointing was He a Son by kingship. Both birth and kingship brought enriched meaning to His eternal sonship. So He was ever God's eternal Son, but, "Thou art My Son," signified He had entered His kingship.

In England, the story is told of a great stone in which was embedded a miraculous sword. No one would be able to draw that sword from the stone except God's chosen king of England. And though the kingdom was in danger of crumbling for lack of a king, it endured and awaited its leader. At last, the man named Arthur came, drew the sword from the stone, and thereby alerted the kingdom that a king was in the land. At Christ's baptism, the first words of the Father's proclamation had done the same.

LAMBS AND PRIESTS

But the Father's next words told the kind of King Jesus was: "My . . . [Beloved] in whom I am well-pleased" (Matt. 3:17). This, too, is a literal quotation from the Old Testament[5] (Isa. 42:1). In fact, it is taken from the beginning of the greatest series of scriptural prophecies about the Christ. In this series, four increasingly descriptive passages paint an astonishing portrait of the true Servant-Christ who contrasts the disobedient servant-nation of Israel. For Christ is gradually revealed as the servant who will suffer deeply in submitting to the will of God (Isa. 42:1-9; 49:1-7; 50:4-9; 52:13—53:12 in contrast to 42:18-21).

The beginning of the first passage, in Isaiah 42:1-4, is quoted by Matthew, in 12:18-21.

> "BEHOLD, MY SERVANT WHOM I HAVE CHOSEN;
> MY BELOVED IN WHOM MY SOUL IS WELL-PLEASED;
> I WILL PUT MY SPIRIT UPON HIM,
> AND HE SHALL PROCLAIM JUSTICE TO THE GENTILES.
> 19"HE WILL NOT QUARREL, NOR CRY OUT;
> NOR WILL ANYONE HEAR HIS VOICE IN THE STREETS.
> 20"A BATTERED REED HE WILL NOT BREAK OFF,
> AND A SMOLDERING WICK HE WILL NOT PUT OUT,
> UNTIL HE LEADS JUSTICE TO VICTORY.
> 21"AND IN HIS NAME THE GENTILES WILL HOPE"
> (Matt. 12:18-21).

The next verse of this passage in Isaiah adds:

> He will not be disheartened or crushed,
> until He has established justice in the earth;
> and the coastlands will wait expectantly for His law.
>   (Isa. 42:4).

In this first passage, His suffering is scarcely noticeable, but it can be perceived if we look closely. In the statement, "He will not cry out," the words "cry out" normally mean "cry out for help."[6] So it appears He will be in danger. Then the assurance that "He will not be disheartened or crushed" seems to imply that He will not only confront danger but overcome tragedy.

In the second passage, that tragedy is more plainly set forth (Isa. 49:1-7). Although He has been prepared by God for a special task (Isa. 49:1-3), He tastes the bitterness of apparent failure. And this failure could bring the words of despair, "I have toiled in vain, I have spent My strength for nothing and [emptiness]" (Isa. 49:4). Yet, at the same time, His faith that God would vindicate Him brings the words of confidence, "Yet surely the justice due to Me is with the LORD, and My reward with My God" (Isa. 49:4). And He affirms this, even in the midst of a failure so severe that He is addressed as "the despised One, . . . the One abhorred by the nation, . . . the Servant of rulers" (Isa. 49:7).

The third passage is even more painfully explicit (Isa. 50:4-9). His suffering is portrayed as cruelly undeserved. He has been trained by God to help the weary with a kind word, to encourage, and to heal. Yet He must say, "I gave My back to those who strike Me, and My cheeks to those who [lay it bare];[7] I did not cover My face from humiliation and spitting" (Isa. 50:6).

The last of these four passages, however, is the most graphic picture yet of His suffering (Isa. 52:14—53:12). Almost every verse reels with His pain; some reek with His blood. "His appearance was marred more than any man, and His form more than the sons of men" (Isa. 52:14). He was "despised," "forsaken," "stricken," "smitten," "pierced through," "crushed," "scourged" (Isa. 53:3-5). He was "like a lamb that is led to slaughter" (Isa. 53:7). And He was "cut off out of the land of the living" (Isa. 53:8).

His death is horribly set before us. Yet it is no ordinary death; it is called a guilt offering (Isa. 53:10). This was one of the sacrifices the ancient Israelites offered to God. Normally, a priest brought the animal for the guilt-offering sacrifice. But here the Servant brings not a lamb but Himself. Now we know why He suffers. It is because His work climaxes in the priestly work of bringing a sacrifice, only the sacrifice is Himself. So the Servant suffers as a priest who brings the unique sacrifice of Himself to the altar.

Thus in the Father's designation of Jesus as the Servant who will bring a sacrifice, He has designated Him as a Priest. He is not only a King, but also a Priest. "Thou art My . . . Son," designated a King; "My . . . [Beloved] in whom I am well-pleased," designated a Priest. And, in retrospect, it should not surprise us that the Father has accented the priesthood and, hence, the death of His Son. For His passing through the judgment waters of death had just been symbolized and foreshadowed in His passing through the judgment waters of His baptism.

LOVE AND LOSS

A third phrase ingeniously results from the apposition of the phrase "[the beloved] in whom I am well-pleased" to the phrase, "This is My [Son]." "[The Beloved]" becomes immediately appositional to "Son," and hence descriptive of it. "Beloved Son" is thus a third significant title of Christ, woven into the Father's proclamation. Some even translate the Father's words as, "This is My beloved Son, in whom I am well-pleased." And that is quite an acceptable translation.

Now, once again, we are faced with a phrase which may appear to be an ordinary one; but if we painstakingly explore the Scripture, we will discover quite the opposite. This term is used only six times, three of those as a title of Isaac, Abraham's "beloved son" (or "only son," as it is rendered in Genesis).[8] And, furthermore, each of those three referring to Isaac occurs in Genesis 22, the chapter in which Abraham is commanded to sacrifice his "beloved son." When we add to all this the fact that, in Jewish first-century culture, Isaac was a well-known example of willing sacrifice,[9] and Christ has been designated a Priest of sacrifice, it seems certain that He has been called a beloved Son in a sense similar to Isaac.

How fascinating this now becomes. After Abraham had

agonizingly waited years for the birth of a son, no father ever loved a son more than he loved Isaac. He had seen him grow almost to manhood. Then came God's incredible command to offer him up in sacrifice.

The struggle within Abraham was beyond description. His heart could scarcely bear to obey. Yet somehow, some way unknown to most of us, he submitted. For he knew two things. First, that God had promised him his descendants would come through Isaac. And second, that Isaac was about to die without descendants.

But Abraham also believed that God would not lie, and, as the New Testament assures us (Heb. 11:17-19), that God would therefore raise Isaac from the dead to give birth to those descendants.

Yet when would Isaac be raised? After one day? One week? A year after Abraham's death? Abraham could not know. He was perhaps never to see Isaac again. No doubt, he spoke little on the appointed day. He rose early, briefly told Isaac of a journey they must take to a mountain named Moriah, and silently prepared to go. Numbly, he gathered the wood of sacrifice; Isaac carried it, not knowing of its use. At last, the horrible, dreadful moment came. Abraham prepared the wood for sacrifice, almost oblivious to his actions. He could think only of his love for Isaac, the loss he anticipated.

But, then, as he lifted the knife which would pierce Isaac's heart and his own soul, God spoke. The knife was withheld. Isaac would not be sacrificed, God said.

For Abraham, the test was over. The knife was sheathed. Abraham had demonstrated his unqualified love for God by this willingness to give up his only son to Him. God would later demonstrate His unqualified love for mankind by His willingness to give up *His* only Son for them. Only then, the knife would not be withheld.

So not only was Jesus designated as a King to reign and a Priest to die, but also as a beloved Son, whose death would demonstrate the unsurpassing love of the Father.

It has been a long journey to this conclusion for us in the twentieth century. For those in the first century, it was not so long. They would know the meaning of the Father's proclamation. But it was said so briefly and quickly. It took time for its significance to sink into their minds. Imagine how the eyes of the crowd turned toward this humble Carpenter from Nazareth. Some squinted in doubt and confusion. Others opened their eyes wide in amazement. Many perhaps winced with the sad look of a child who has nearly always been disappointed but is still trying to hope. Then some succeeded in hoping, and a look of peace came upon their faces, as they gazed toward heaven, whence the voice had come. And they realized at last, that after centuries of endless waiting, God's Son and King and Priest was in the land.

So the Father had declared at the Jordan, when Jesus humbled Himself to be baptized. A beloved Son destined to die. A life-saving Priest with no lamb of sacrifice but Himself. A mighty King clad in carpenter's clothes. But clothes He would wear, until His mission of sacrifice was accomplished. He had accepted that mission at the Jordan. The course of His life was set.

3

THE WILDERNESS OF CONFLICT

There is one story that Virtue has her dwelling place above rock walls hard to climb with a grave chorus of light-footed nymphs attendant about her, and she is not to be looked upon by the eyes of every mortal, only by one who with sweat, with clenched concentration and courage, climbs to the peak.[1]

Simonides of Ceos, sixth century B.C.

The heroic pattern began with a time of choice; it proceeded with a time of testing. It was inevitable that it should have been so. How else would this Hero have foreshadowed His greater victories? How else, indeed, would He have trained for them, if not by strenuous testing? Hercules, for example, even as an infant, struggled with deadly snakes. And every athlete, in the professional arena, has known first the testing of boyhood athletics and agonizing practice.

Very agonizing practice, which is performed away from the arena and the crowds, and is seldom appreciated, except by those who know from their own experience the high cost of competitive conditioning. This physical testing is neither endured nor known by many. Yet there is a spiritual testing, endured and known by fewer still.

Thus it was in the life of the Hero from Nazareth. Training and testing, sweat and ache. Not a struggle from sin to virtue, for He was sinless; but an endurance from one experience of obedience to a deeper one. However, that could happen only if He were in the midst of deeper difficulty, in a place where the cost of obedience was much higher than in the coolness of Galilee or the occasional refreshment of the Jordan valley. In the desert of Israel—called the wilderness—the testing would come. This would be His training and would prepare Him for the path His life would follow.

Milton expressed the purpose of the wilderness testing in the following words, as though spoken by God the Father.

But first I mean
To exercise Him in the wilderness;
There He shall first lay down the rudiments
Of His great warfare, ere I send Him forth
To conquer Sin and Death the two grand foes,
By Humiliation and Strong Sufference.[2]

These are lines from *Paradise Regained,* an appropriate title. For if Jesus would succeed in the wilderness, He could proceed on to a victory which would secure paradise for those who belonged to Him.

THE RECORD OF CONFLICT

This wilderness testing is succinctly recorded by Matthew:

Then Jesus was led up by the Spirit into the wilderness to be tempted by the devil. [2]And after He had fasted forty days and forty nights, He then became hungry. [3]And the tempter came and said to Him, "If You are the Son of God, command that these stones become bread." [4]But He answered and said, "It is written, 'MAN SHALL NOT LIVE ON BREAD ALONE, BUT ON EVERY WORD THAT PROCEEDS OUT OF THE MOUTH OF GOD.' " [5]Then the devil took Him into the holy city; and he stood Him on the pinnacle of the Temple, [6]and said to Him, "If You are the Son of God throw Yourself down; for it is written, 'HE WILL GIVE HIS ANGELS CHARGE CONCERNING YOU; AND ON THEIR

HANDS THEY WILL BEAR YOU UP, LEST YOU STRIKE YOUR FOOT AGAINST A STONE.' " [7]Jesus said to him, "On the other hand, it is written, 'YOU SHALL NOT TEMPT THE LORD YOUR GOD.' " [8]Again, the devil took Him to a very high mountain, and showed Him all the kingdoms of the world, and their glory; [9]and he said to Him, "All these things will I give You, if You fall down and worship me." [10]Then Jesus said to him, "Begone, Satan! For it is written, 'YOU SHALL WORSHIP THE LORD YOUR GOD, AND SERVE HIM ONLY.' " [11]Then the devil left Him; and behold, angels came and began to minister to Him (Matt. 4:1-11).

THE HOT WINDS OF DEATH

The wilderness was an arena of conflict unsurpassed in the testing of any other hero. It was, first of all, the opponent's home territory—Satan's specially designed playing field. This desolate, deathly region was rightfully known as the place of the curse of God.[3] On the other hand, God's blessing was represented by inhabited, cultivated land. But in the desert wilderness, there was neither tree, fruit, nor growth—only wild, unwanted beasts whose shrieks seemed to rise from hell itself.

In the opening scene of *The Exorcist*, an archaeological site in northern Iraq captures this mood of the wilderness. It is a remarkable sight. The huge setting sun seems to rest like a gigantic fireball on the desert. A statue of an idol is on one side; the archaeologist-priest is on the other, and they face each other in conflict. In the foreground, two vicious dogs tear at each other's throats. And, quite ingeniously, this symbolism is from the eighteenth "Greater Trump" card of the Tarot deck used by fortunetellers. It is said to symbolize the conditions of hell. The scene is ominous, dreadful, heavy, and oppressive with the weight of the evil it signifies.

That was the kind of desert in which Jesus was tested.

That was the kind of evil He faced, but not its representation in idolatrous images or fighting dogs. He faced the dreadful reality of Satan himself—the tempter and devil, as the passage also calls him. He deserved each title: "Satan," because it means "adversary" or "opposer," and he opposed Jesus in His mission; "devil," because it means "slanderer," and he plainly slandered and questioned the name of the Son of God; "tempter," because he is the source of so much temptation and sought to entice Jesus to sin. By using these three titles, the Scripture seems to be telling us that every diabolical aspect of Satan's character and work will confront the Lord Jesus in the evil of the wilderness.

The Dove Like an Eagle

But, in one sense, He would not face it alone. Matthew tells us that God the Holy Spirit had led Him to this place (4:1). And Luke adds that this same Holy Spirit provided Jesus with overflowing inner strength to aid Him against the tempter (Luke 4:1). The Spirit had come upon Jesus like a dove, but He indwelt Him with the strength of an eagle. So the presence of the Holy Spirit was indeed with Him. Yet, in another sense, Jesus *was* alone against Satan. For the attack was aimed directly against Him and His task. Thus, in the strength that God the Holy Spirit supplied, the Son of God set out for the wilderness to be alone before the Father. And there, before He faced the ordeal of the devil's temptations, He fasted forty days and nights.

Reflections from the Jordan Waters

Why did He fast? Physical weakness from fasting would presumably give the evil one an extra advantage in the combat. For a weakened body frequently brings a weakened will. Yet the fasting was necessary—not to begin the conflict but to conclude the purpose of His baptism.

Throughout the Old Testament, fasting was the most common outward form of repentance.[4] And we have already discovered that Jesus was baptized in repentance—not for His own sin, of course, but for the sin of Israel. The fasting in the wilderness was therefore the outward expression of the repentance He expressed at the baptism.

The testing was directly related to the event of baptism, too. For at the baptism, He was declared God's Son, and now this testing would confirm His worthiness of that title. No sooner did the Father declare, "Thou art my . . . Son," than Satan would have Him cast doubt on that proclamation. "If You are the Son of God," he mockingly said, "then let us see something more than a tired, hungry man alone in the desert. Turn stones into bread; leap from the pinnacle of the Temple into the arms of angels; rule all the kingdoms of the earth." Yet Jesus demonstrated His true sonship by continued obedience to the will of the Father. So the testing would indeed deepen the reality of His sonship by a deeper experience of the obedience of sonship.

Every follower of Christ can expect a similar experience. No sooner will the Scriptures declare him a Christian because of his faith in Christ than Satan will come to cast doubt on his conversion. The tempter intends to confuse a new believer, but God designs the test to deepen the reality of his faith. Or farther down the road of Christian maturity, a believer may be given responsibility in the Christian community, and once again Satan will inflict his barbs. Satan wants the testing to cause that one to doubt his appointment for service, but God plans it to make the tested one dependent upon His sufficiency to accomplish the task.

The trial may be severe and, as in the case of Christ's

testing, all of Satan's schemes may be brought to bear against a believer. But as Christ was empowered by the Holy Spirit for inner spiritual strength, so every believer in Christ is indwelt by the Holy Spirit for the same purpose (Rom. 8:9). Nevertheless, a careful understanding of Satan's strategy in the wilderness could help prepare us all for such a conflict.

THE BEGINNING OF COMBAT

In the first test, the tempter said to Him, "If You are the Son of God, command that these stones become bread." But Jesus answered him, "It is written, 'MAN SHALL NOT LIVE ON BREAD ALONE, BUT ON EVERY WORD THAT PROCEEDS OUT OF THE MOUTH OF GOD' " (Matt. 4:3-4).

In order to understand the significance of the temptation, we must understand the meaning of Jesus' reply. Jesus' response is frequently understood to mean something like: "Man lives not only by literal bread but also by spiritual bread, and now is the time for spiritual food." The application would be that one's quiet time before God is more important than his breakfast. And while that may be a valid principle, I do not believe it reflects the meaning of Jesus' particular reply or the nature of Satan's temptation.

Jesus had quoted a portion of Moses' speech, in Deuteronomy 8:3, in this context: "[God] humbled you and let you be hungry, then fed you with manna which you had never seen nor had your fathers seen, that He might teach you that man does not live by bread alone, but man lives by everything that proceeds out of the mouth of God." As God had spoken the world into existence at creation, so He later spoke other things within creation into existence too, including the food of manna for the people of Israel in the wilderness. Hence, that literal bread could be said to have proceeded from the mouth of God, for the word that created it proceeded from His mouth. And, consequently, that manna was not bread "alone," but bread directly from God.

God was teaching Israel that the daily needs of life are met, not in a manner unrelated to Him and "alone," but by the daily provisions of His providence, proceeding from His creative word. He taught them in a very effective way. First, He let them be hungry and aware of their need. Then He miraculously fed them, so they would learn that their daily food came from Him. It was ingeniously simple. And Christ, also, had learned the lesson well. His food would come in the Father's time and in the Father's way.

When Satan challenged Christ to make bread from stones, He replied that He would wait for the bread the Father would give Him. "MAN SHALL NOT LIVE ON BREAD 'ALONE' "—independent of God—"BUT ON EVERY WORD THAT PROCEEDS OUT OF THE MOUTH OF GOD," including the word which creates daily bread. Though He was hungry, and it was right to eat, yet He would not eat independently of the Father's will. Satan had tempted Him not away from spiritual bread but away from the Father and toward literal bread, gained independently of the Father's will.

In a similar manner, he will also tempt us. Food, for example, may be a legitimate bodily need. Scripture includes sex as a legitimate bodily need as well. But both of these God-instilled needs must be met by means He has approved. Food should not be stolen, and sex should not be adulterous. Legitimate needs must be met by legitimate means. This the Lord Jesus knew, and this He showed by hungering more to do the Father's will than to eat the bread of Satan's table. And, by so doing, He left for us the example to hunger and thirst after righteousness to the same degree.

But Satan tempts by other means than physical needs. So we must observe, with equal care, Jesus' response to a second test. Whereas the first temptation appealed to a personal need, the second offered the prize of public recognition. And a very special sort of recognition it was.

Satan stood Christ upon the pinnacle of the Temple in the center of Jerusalem and challenged Him to cast Himself from it. "Does the Scripture not say," Satan asked, "that the angels of God would miraculously save You?" The clever tempter even quoted Psalm 91:11-12 to prove it. Had Christ performed such an astonishing act, the effect would have been widespread. In all likelihood, this kind of miraculous political stunt before the crowds in the capital city would have brought Jesus recognition as the national Messiah,[5] the Son of David designated by God to rule over the nation. It was, in fact, a recognition He deserved. But it would not have been gained by means the Father approved.

"YE SHALL NOT [PUT TO THE TEST] THE LORD YOUR GOD," Jesus replied. There is a difference, He knew, between faith and presumption. He would not leap from the Temple and place His Father in a position where He was compelled to act miraculously on His Son's behalf. To do so would be an implicit rejection of the Father's right to determine the time and place of His miracles. So the Son intended to serve the Father, not force miracles from His hand.

In this attitude, He once again left us an example to follow. Had He chosen to pray for angels to save Him, He would have ended His prayer with, "if it be Thy will." For he recognized that prayer is a request, and, like all requests, it may be either granted or denied. But had He leaped from the Temple, He would not have requested but demanded that the angels save Him. And He refused to "[PUT TO THE TEST] THE LORD [HIS] GOD." If He were to ask the Father to act, He would wait for the Father to answer.

Similarly, we also should regard our prayer requests of the Father. We must never imagine that we can say certain magical words which force God to serve us. As children speaking to their Father, we must realize He is free to grant or deny the requests we make. Of course, some requests He has already promised to answer. He has promised forgiveness, for example, to everyone who asks with faith in Christ. But even a request like this, which He has already promised to answer, is not granted because we say magical words, but because we ask in faith. The other requests we make, which He has not explicitly promised to answer, we must leave to His wisdom and timing—even requests for things altogether necessary and appropriate.

This was Christ's attitude. As it was right for Him to eat bread, so it was right for Him to be honored as the Messiah. Yet it would have been wrong to do either by means apart from the Father's will. The time would come when the miraculous creation of bread to feed thousands, and His recognition as Messiah to rule millions would serve the Father's will. But this was not the time, nor were Satan's suggestions the means, to do either.

We often face similar temptations. For example, the need of companionship in marriage, of recognition in one's profession, or of completeness in the birth of children to one's family are all unquestionably legitimate desires. But the timing and means of their achievement rest with the Father. One should not marry an unsuitable partner, choose recognition of men over approval from God, or grow bitterly impatient over the absence of children. The prayer for all these must be laid before the Father. Then the responsible activity one exerts for their attainment must be pleasing to Him, too. At last, when the goals are reached, as when the bread was created or Messianic honor was received, one will be thankful to the Father for His work.

FINAL STRATEGY

The account of the last temptation reinforces this principle and builds upon it. In this last test, all the kingdoms of the earth are offered to Christ by Satan. And these kingdoms, like the bread and Messianic recognition, were destined by God to be His. The bread was necessary for His life; the recognition was intended for His rule; the kingdoms were guaranteed by right of inheritance. For what son does not inherit the possessions of his father? By God the earth had been made; to the Son of God it would belong. Thus, in each temptation, Satan offered a prize the Son of God was intended to possess. But how clear it now becomes that the means for receiving those prizes from Satan entailed a rejection of the Father's will.

"If You will fall down and worship me," Satan added, "You may have the world." This blunt proposal served only to unmask for us the evil already crystal clear to Christ from the previous proposals. What had been subtly disguised is now blatantly plain. Satan had all along been asking Christ to act independently of the Father. And whether this were done by the seemingly harmless creation of bread, or the obviously sinful worship of Satan, the result would be essentially the same. One step may have been short and the other long, but each was away from the Father.

It seems incredible that an intelligent being, even a disobedient one like Satan, would think that so obvious an enticement to evil could succeed against the Son of God. I can only offer a suggestion which might explain it. After thousands of years of tempting others, Satan had no doubt learned that the greater the prize for one's sin, the greater was one's willingness to commit it. Few women, for example, would consent to prostitution, but how many would commit adultery once for a million dollars? Few men would like the reputation of a liar, but how many would lie just once to quadruple their salary or win the girl they loved? So perhaps Satan considered the greatness of owning all the kingdoms of the earth to be an offer no one could refuse.

But it was refused. "YOU SHALL WORSHIP THE LORD YOUR GOD, AND SERVE HIM ONLY" was Christ's response. And if we are to imitate the Son of God, we must respond in a similar manner.

THE VICTOR'S PRIZE

After this victory, it is written that the angels of God ministered to Him. It was not the right time for angels to care for Him when Satan challenged Him to cast Himself from the Temple, but now it was time for angels to serve Him. And by now dispatching His angels, God the Father implicitly reaffirmed the sonship He had declared at the baptism. Satan had said, "Leap from the Temple and force God to send His angels and prove You're His Son, the Messiah." But Jesus left the time of reaffirmation in the Father's hands. Then having submitted to the Father, He was approved and exalted by the Father at the proper time.

When we are obedient in the midst of difficulty, we can anticipate the same reward—God's approval and affirmation that we have acted like His sons and daughters.

A DECATHLON OF TESTING

If the testing of Christ is representative, however, we must be warned that our testing will be comprehensive, too. Notice how thoroughly He was tested. With respect to His titles as Son of God, Son of David, and Son of

Abraham, each temptation consecutively challenged Him. As the Son of God, in His humanity needing daily bread, He was tempted to create food independently of the Father; as Son of David, anointed to reign over Israel, He was tempted to national recognition by the independent performance of a miraculous political stunt; as the Son of Abraham, destined to rule the earth, He was tempted to gain all the kingdoms of the earth by the worship of Satan. So He was tested in each role implied by His major titles.

Each role had a progressively wider influence, also, like expanding concentric circles. The first was in the personal realm; the second, the national realm; the third, the international realm. So we can expect Satan to test us in our activities, both personal and widespread, too.

Jesus was also tested in each kind of relationship possible. In the temptation of food, He was tested in His selfward relationship. In the temptation to public recognition, He was tested in His manward relationship. And in the temptation to worship Satan, He was tested in His Godward relationship. Some may regard this from a different perspective as a testing in the realm of body, soul, and spirit. But however they are regarded, it is easy to see how completely His relationships were tested.

Finally, if we accept John's classifications of sin as "the desire of the flesh, the desire of the eye, and the pride of possessions"[6] (1 John 2:16, NIV), we will recognize that He was tested in each category. Food appealed to the "desire of the flesh." National recognition appealed to the "desire of the eye" upon others' admiration and approval. All the kingdoms of the earth explicitly appealed to the "pride of possessions." The Lord Jesus faced comprehensive testings, and His followers may expect similar ones to confront them too. However, they should hope to imitate Christ, not only by experiencing the same kind of testings

He faced, but also by seeking to follow the triumph He left as an example.

Unveiling the Scene in the Wilderness

However, His victory is much more than an example. The story of it is woven from the threads of the larger fabric of the entire Scripture. Only by tracing these threads back to their origin and forward to their end, can we fully understand the depth and breadth of the meaning of His victory. The temptation account is but one frame in the film of revelation begun in the Old Testament and continued in the New. To fully appreciate the one frame, we must first view the earlier portion of the film so that we can understand the background to the frame. And as various backgrounds highlight different colors in a multicolored fabric, so various backgrounds from the Old Testament highlight different aspects of the multifaceted meaning of His victory.

Important events are often like this. Imagine, for example, that you are viewing a large, partially veiled picture, of which you can see only two central figures crossing a finish line in a race. You may notice that the runner in the American uniform has defeated the one in a Russian uniform. So you know, at least, that an American has defeated a Russian in track competition.

But suppose the picture is unveiled further, and you see that contestants from other countries had entered the race, too. Then you would know that this winner had won a very important race with international competition. Now suppose at last the picture is completely unveiled, and you see the Olympic symbols over the stadium and thousands of fans from all over the world. Then you would have seen this event in its broadest perspective and understood that not only had the winner defeated his arch rival and won where others had failed, but he also had achieved a victory of worldwide importance. We shall also draw these precise conclusions when we set the victory of Christ against the background of the Old Testament.

SHADOW OF ANOTHER BATTLE

This initial victory of the last and eternal Davidic King was pictured long beforehand by the initial victory of the first Davidic king, David himself. The patterns of victory were remarkably similar. Just as Jesus was anointed in the presence of the prophet John before His reception of the Spirit and subsequent testing, so David was anointed in the presence of the prophet Samuel before his reception of the Spirit and subsequent testing (1 Sam. 16). Then as Jesus next went to the wilderness to face the devil, who had been oppressing the nation of Israel for centuries, so David, in the next chapter after his anointing, went to the valley of Elah to face the nine-foot Goliath, the greatest Philistine warrior who had been oppressing the nation of Israel, too. Perhaps most remarkably, whereas forty days lapsed before the actual confrontation began for Jesus, so the Scripture tells us that "the Philistine [Goliath] came forward morning and evening for forty days, and took his stand" against Israel (1 Sam. 17:16).

So forty days set the stage for the battle of each with an enemy of Israel. And each defeated that enemy by dependence upon the power of God. When we set the test of Christ against the background of David's victory in the valley of Elah, we see a small portion of the picture unveiled. Like the viewer who saw only the one American defeat the Russian in a race, we learn at least that our divine Competitor has defeated an arch rival of His people.

Matthew would prefer that we set the temptation against a broader background, however. Although it is perhaps not always observed, Matthew's gospel is indeed a fascinating work of art, in which he deliberately compares and contrasts the life of Christ with the history of Israel.

Think about it for a moment. The nation began with a supernatural birth (Deut. 32:18). As a small company of seventy persons, the nation went down into Egypt during the time of Joseph. Years later, under the direction of Moses, they left Egypt as a multitude and crossed the Red Sea. For forty years, they remained in the wilderness, where they underwent testing. During this time, they received the law from Mount Sinai through Moses who, in Deuteronomy, applied this Law to their experiences in the wilderness and commanded its obedience in the future.

After laying this foundation for the nation, much of Old Testament history can be sketched as alternative periods of teaching (1400-1000 B.C.), miracles (Elijah and Elisha), and teaching (800-400 B.C. under the prophets). And in these proclamations of the prophets, the history concludes with the two grand themes of condemnation and consolation. The just condemnation of the nation and their dominance by other nations would continue until the Messiah came. But with His appearing, the gracious consolation would be the glorious resurrection of the nation in the future under the Messiah.

Matthew found it easy to set the history of the Messiah against the history of Israel. Jesus also began with a supernatural birth, was taken to Egypt when young, was brought from Egypt to Israel, and fulfilled the pattern of the nation's history to such a degree that Matthew could apply words about the nation to words about the Son. "OUT OF EGYPT DID I CALL MY SON"(Matt. 2:15; Hos.

11:1)—true of the national son and true of the Messianic One. As the nation then crossed the Red Sea waters of judgment, so Christ next passed through the Jordan waters of judgment, and then, like the nation, proceeded to the wilderness—the nation for forty years, the Son for forty days.

Whereas the nation received the Old Covenant Law from Mount Sinai during this time, Jesus soon gave His law in the Sermon on the Mount (Matt. 5-7). Then much of Matthew's account, like Old Testament history, revolved around times of miracles and teaching. And as the history of Israel had concluded upon the themes of their just condemnation and gracious resurrection in the future, Matthew provided a remarkable contrast as he concluded with the unjust condemnation of the righteous Son, followed by a resurrection which vindicated Him.

Finally, whereas the nation, as a disobedient servant of God, failed to take the revelation of God to the world (Isa. 42:18-21), Matthew recorded Christ's great commission to the disciples to take the gospel to all nations.

CHRIST, ISRAEL, AND THE WILDERNESS

In light of the broad background of Israel's history, it should not surprise us if, when we look more carefully at Matthew's account of the testing of Christ, we should discover it is very particularly set against the testing of Israel. We have already observed that as the nation entered their forty years of testing after crossing the Red Sea, so Jesus entered His forty days of testing after passing through the Jordan. But the similarities go much farther.

BREAD AND FAITH

One might recall that in response to Satan's first test Jesus quoted Deuteronomy 8:3, "MAN SHALL NOT LIVE ON BREAD ALONE, BUT ON EVERY WORD THAT PROCEEDS OUT OF

THE MOUTH OF GOD." A closer look at this quotation reveals that it is a lesson drawn by Moses directly from Israel's first test over lack of food.[7] No sooner had Israel sung praises in the song of Moses for God's deliverance from Egypt (Exod. 15:1-18) and observed His capacity to provide for their need of water (15:22-27), than they grumbled over their lack of bread and meat (16:1-3).

The Lord Jesus evidently knew of their faithless response, and also of the lesson Moses drew from it. Jesus, therefore, determined to respond—not as faithless Israel had, but as Moses had commanded. Israel rebelled against God and accused Him of bringing them to the wilderness to kill them. Jesus submitted to God and entrusted His life to the Father He knew would sustain Him.

So His first response is an instructive contrast to the nation's. It is also a model for us. We should not accuse God of trying to kill us every time we encounter hardship. Such an experience is intended not to curse but to bless us, as it blessed the Lord Jesus when He responded in faith.

ANGELS AND MIRACLES

But we should contrast the nation's response in the next temptation, too. In response to Satan's second test, Jesus quoted Deuteronomy 6:16, "YOU SHALL NOT [PUT TO THE TEST] THE LORD YOUR GOD." This quotation, like Jesus' first one, is taken from a lesson taught by Moses drawn from one of Israel's tests. And that test, quite interestingly, was the very next one the people experienced after their lack of food. After applying the lesson drawn from Israel's response to their lack of food, in Exodus 16, Jesus prepared for His second test by arming Himself with the lesson drawn from Israel's second test, in Exodus 17. With that lesson given by Moses, in Deuteronomy 6:16, Jesus would answer Satan. What could more clearly set His testing against the background of Israel's?

Only His response could do so, for it dramatically contrasted their own. They were tempted to put God to the test when they were faced with lack of water, in Exodus 17. Once again, they cried out that God intended to kill them, when, on the contrary, He intended the trial to increase their faith. On the other hand, when Jesus was challenged to put God to the test by Satan, He refused to do so and continued to entrust Himself to the Father.

KINGDOMS AND IDOLS

The superiority of Christ's character continued to manifest itself in the final test. In His response to the last temptation, He quoted Deuteronomy 6:13, "YOU SHALL WORSHIP THE LORD YOUR GOD, AND SERVE HIM ONLY." This, in the context, is an explicit command to reject idolatry, a practice regarded in Scripture as equivalent to the worship of Satan and his demons (1 Cor. 10:19-20). Yet this was precisely what Israel practiced in the wilderness. And quite significantly, Matthew recorded their idolatry as the temptation and failure which next followed the first two tests with which Christ's have been compared.[8]

A remarkable contrast again results. In their third test, the nation bowed before the golden calf for the mere hope that this idol would bring them to their land. Yet Christ refused to bow to Satan, even were the tempter to bring Him the world.

It now becomes clear that the three quotations with which Christ repelled Satan's three tests in the wilderness were lessons drawn previously by Moses from three successive tests of Israel in the wilderness. In each case, Christ's faith stood in contrast to their unbelief; His submission, to their rebellion; His worship with their idolatry. But He had not merely succeeded where they had failed. He had also foreshadowed a success where they had failed in the world.

CONTRAST COMPLETE

Israel had been predominantly a disobedient servant which had not extended blessing to the nations of the earth. The Lord Jesus Christ, however, would, by His obedience even to death, bring that long awaited blessing to the nations. The responsibility for the proclamation of it would then be given to the disciples. Thus, when Matthew concluded his gospel with that global commission, he had shown a fulfillment of what he foreshadowed in the wilderness testing. Christ indeed succeeded where Israel failed.

Matthew unveiled the portrait of the temptation enough to give his readers that perspective. It was like the unveiling of the imaginary picture of the race in which the American runner is seen to have defeated not only an arch rival but even runners from other countries, too. From this broader perspective, the viewer would thus see the deeper significance of the same race. Matthew gives us that broader view of the temptation which gives it a deeper significance, too.

THE WIDE ANGLE LENS OF LUKE

The perspective from Luke, however, is broader still. He unveiled the portrait of the temptation completely. It is as if he further unveiled the picture of the race and revealed the Olympic symbols over the stadium and thousands cheering for the world's new gold medalist. Luke exposed to view these Olympic symbols over the stadium of the temptation by skillfully placing Christ's temptation in the wilderness against the background of Adam's temptation in the garden.

After surveying Luke's gospel, we should not be surprised by this perspective. More than any other gospel writer he focused on individuals. For example, whereas the parables cited by Matthew normally focused on the kingdom, the parables recorded by Luke focused upon individuals. And in the narrative history itself, Luke again centered upon individuals and gave us not only the fullest descriptions of those persons who are mentioned in the other gospels, but also included and sometimes described persons passed over by the other writers. Luke skillfully brought to the stage of his history people like the priest Zacharias, the cousins Elizabeth and Mary, the sisters Mary and Martha, the tax-collector Zaccheus, the disappointed Cleopas, and many others. He did not confine description to men either. Thirteen times he spoke of women not mentioned by the other writers. Luke was indeed interested in individuals.

New Testament students have observed that he was also especially interested in the universal scope of Christ's influence.[9] For example, the angels' good-will message was directed not to a few but to every man on the earth with whom God is pleased (Luke 2:14). Or again, the record of John the Baptist's preaching added a universal declaration that Matthew omitted: "ALL FLESH SHALL SEE THE SALVATION OF GOD" (Luke 3:6).

When we join his interest in individuals with his interest in Christ's universal significance, the background from Adam's testing becomes quite plausible. For he, too, was an individual whose test carried universal significance. Now when we remember that Luke was a traveling companion and student of Paul, and Paul, more than any other author of the New Testament, stressed the contrast of Adam and Christ (Rom. 5:12-21; 1 Cor. 15:22, 45-47), Luke's contrast of Christ's temptation with Adam's becomes almost expected.

A more careful look at his account confirms that expectation. And he painted the background of Adam behind the temptation account by—of all things—a fascinating and artistic use of the genealogy of Christ. First, unlike Matthew who traced Christ only to Abraham, Luke traced His descent all the way to Adam. Next, to focus attention upon this descent to Adam, he placed the genealogy not at the beginning of his gospel where it would be expected, but as a transition between the account of the baptism and the temptation. Then, to particularly highlight Adam, Luke did not begin with him and go forward in time to Christ, as was commonly done, but he began with Christ and descended back in time to Adam. The ingenious result was that the name of Adam was placed precisely before the temptation account.

Perhaps the skill of Luke is seen best in one last effect of his genealogy, which even more definitely set Adam in contrast to Christ. Notice that in a very real sense, he traced Christ's descent not merely to Adam but to God, for he proceeded as follows: "Jesus . . . being supposedly the son of Joseph, the son of Eli, the son of Matthat. . . . the son of Seth, the son of Adam, the son of God"[10] (Luke 3:23-24, 38). In a most subtle way, Luke has given the title "son of God" a significant new sense.

The title has occasionally been given to Israel corporately (Hos. 11:1), the Davidic king individually (2 Sam. 7:12-16), Christ because of His divine birth (Luke 1:35), because of His Messiahship (Matt. 3:17), or because of eternal sonship (Matt. 28:19). It also rests upon Christians, because they are adopted into God's family (Gal. 3:26). But only in Luke 3:38 does it mean simply "the direct offspring of God." And only two persons will ever qualify for that sense of the title—not Eve, for she was created from man—but only Adam the first man, and Christ the God-Man.

In fact, Luke included this special sense of the title within its broader usage, when he recorded the reason for the angelic assignment of the title to Christ as being His birth from God (Luke 1:35). So only Adam and Christ were given this special sense of the title, and Adam was given it immediately before the testing of Christ. Both were sons of God; both were tested. Luke could scarcely have more deliberately invited us to compare the results.[11]

Of course, when we examine Satan's strategy against Adam, we must begin with its inception against Eve. For through her, the tempter would reach this man whose choice would shape the future of humanity.

Luke could not have given more signposts from the context to guide his readers into a comparison of the testings. But he did offer one more signpost, not from the context but from within the account itself. By arranging the temptations in a topical sequence rather than a chronological one like Matthew's, Luke consequently could place the third temptation second and the second temptation third. A casual reader might simply observe that Luke had chosen a topical sequence, but a more careful reader will discover why he did so.

It even more effectively placed his account of the temptation against the background of the one in Genesis. With Luke's new sequence, Christ's second temptation will now more easily correspond to Satan's second tactic against Eve. So with the skillful stroke of the artist's brush, Luke has confirmed our conclusion that behind the testing of Christ in the wilderness, he has painted a background of Adam and Eve in paradise.

Consider the parallels which that background illuminates. Jesus was first tested by a lack of food. It was the Father's will that He not eat for a time. And in both Christ's case and that of Eve, Satan questioned the Father's will in his initial strategy. To capture his attitude, we might paraphrase his words to Christ like this, "Has the God who said, 'Thou art My Son,' also said, 'Thou shalt not eat'? How could it be the Father's will that You do not eat? Make bread from stones if You really are the Son of God."

Of course, his words were merely a diabolical echo from the Garden, when he first said to Eve, "Indeed, has God said, 'You shall not eat from any tree of the garden'?" (Gen. 3:1) But whereas Eve began to doubt God, Christ steadfastly continued to trust His Father.

So Satan tried a different tactic. He proceeded from subtly questioning the word of God to outrightly denying it, "Fall down and worship me," he blatantly urged, "and I will give You all the kingdoms of the earth." Thus did his explicit enticement to idolatry blatantly contradict the commandment of God. However, it was the same kind of explicit denial of God's word seen in his second tactic against Eve. "You surely shall not die," he persuasively assured her (Gen. 3:4). But whereas Eve trusted the serpent, Christ repelled him with the same word of God which Eve had forsaken.

Satan employed one last tactic. In Luke's record of the third temptation, Satan tempted Christ to a miraculous proof of His messiahship and national recognition. The admiration of all His countrymen would be His. Although the correspondence to Satan's third tactic against Eve is not as obvious as the others, similarities do exist. In his third tactic against Eve, he also offered great personal ʒain. He promised her a knowledge of good and evil which would make her like God. And, at last, she submitted to Satan. When she saw the fruit "was good for food, and that it was a delight to the eyes, and . . . desirable to make one wise" (Gen. 3:6), she ate the fruit, Scripture says, and Adam soon did, too.

Nevertheless, that very same attractiveness seen by Eve was rejected by Christ. For although He realized that the bread would be good for food, the kingdoms of the earth were a delight to the eyes, and national recognition was desirable to elevate Him at least as high as wisdom would have elevated Eve, He did not submit. Jesus not only succeeded where Israel had failed; he also succeeded where Adam had failed.

And Luke intended that we see this. For the victory of Christ foreshadowed an influence precisely the opposite of Adam's failure. Whereas death entered the world through Adam, life would come to the world through Christ (Rom. 5:12). His death, in place of others and for their sins, would bring this life. So whereas when Adam failed, he dragged the whole human race into his failure; when Christ succeeded, He brought whoever trusts in Him into His success. Adam, beginning in paradise, would ultimately bring a wilderness to the world; Christ, beginning in the wilderness, would ultimately bring a paradise to the world. Luke has indeed lifted the veil from the temptation account and revealed its ultimate significance.

THE BATTLE PLAN

The Scriptures' various perspectives obviously intended that we learn everything possible from Christ's initial victory over Satan. Perhaps we would be unwise if we did not also observe the means by which that victory was accomplished. It is frequently said that Christ defeated Satan by quoting Scripture; therefore, we should memorize Scripture to quote in the midst of our temptations. But the simple reciting of Scripture was in no way a sufficient means of victory for Christ, and neither will it be for us. The Son of God did not merely memorize Scripture and even keenly understand it. He submitted to it from the heart. And so must we, if we intend to follow Him.

But one last thing must be remembered. Apart from the same help He received, we cannot imitate the victory He won. At the very beginning of the temptation account, we are informed that Christ was led and strengthened by the Holy Spirit. Only His help will complete the conditions necessary for our victory in spiritual struggles. Even Satan himself will not defeat the ones in whom the Word and the Spirit are united in a willing heart.

For Casualties in Action

The facts of reality, of course, are that no one besides Christ has ever succeeded in completely submitting to the Father's will. Not that we should fail to try, for by seeking to imitate the Son, we will grow in our relationship with God. However, to enter that relationship with God, we must be forgiven, and that necessitates not a seeking to imitate Christ's success in the wilderness, but a trusting in Christ's victory on the cross. And even after entering the relationship, we must continually depend upon that victory. For as we seek to imitate the obedience of Christ, our failure to do so will daily draw us to Him for forgiveness.

Thankfully, we can know with certainty that He will have compassion upon our weaknesses and understand our failures. For He knows the strength of temptation even better than we. Why? Because He experienced its full force, whereas we often give in before we feel a fraction of it. Hence, the Scripture assures us that "We do not have a high priest who cannot sympathize with our weaknesses, but one who has been tempted in all things as we are, yet without sin. Let us therefore draw near with confidence to the throne of grace, that we may receive mercy and may find grace to help in time of need. . . . Since He Himself was [tested] in that which He has suffered, He is able to come to the aid of those who are [tested]" (Heb. 4:15-16; 2:18).

4

THE MOUNTAIN OF SPLENDOR

But when Aragorn arose all that beheld him gazed in silence, for it seemed to them that he was revealed to them now for the first time. Tall as the sea kings of old, he stood above all that were near, ancient of days he seemed and yet in the flower of manhood; and wisdom sat upon his brow, and strength and healing were in his hands, and a light was about him. And then Faramir cried: "Behold the King."

J. R. R. Tolkien, *The Lord of the Rings,*
Vol. 3, *The Return of the King*

The wilderness of conflict was two years past. The days since had been filled with work, sweat, success, and disappointment. Healing the sick, confronting religious officials, teaching the crowds, and training the disciples had merged the many days into a continuous whole of strenuous activity and intensity. The disciples had heard much from Christ. In fact, they had heard and seen so much, they could scarcely retain a fraction of it. But three specially selected disciples were about to see, on a mountain horizon, a revelation so dazzling they could never forget it.

Upon this mountain, Christ's appearance was transformed into a startling brilliance. It seemed as if His form were outlined with lightning and filled with the sun. His radiant brightness commanded such reality that it made even the fresh, vivid mountain plateau seem like a dull, cardboard image beside Him.

It was an incomparable revelation of the Messiah. For as the immortal God of the universe, He had possessed such glory forever. And thus, He revealed His divinity. But as the resurrected Messianic King, destined to rule the earth, He would display this glory once again. And thus, He also disclosed His destiny. A veil had come over His glory when He clothed Himself with humanity. But the momentary lifting of that veil revealed who He truly was—the incarnate God who would rule the earth.

So His dazzling brilliance cast its rays in two opposite directions. Backward in time, they flashed with the speed of light, on and on infinitely to eternity past where as the eternal Son, He had always dwelt. Yet forward the rays of this glory would shimmer its light across the stage of history, until they signaled the dawning of His righteous kingdom. Thus did the splendrous transformation emblazon His origin and destiny across the mountain sky and reveal His true identity in an unforgettable way.

But why this splendor now? And why show it so briefly? Why not display it before the crowds He taught, or the opposition who doubted? Why did the Father wait until now to so glorify the Son? To answer these questions, we need to investigate the circumstances that preceded the event. They are the key that unlocks the meaning of the event and the answers to these questions.

A TIME OF REVELATION

We discover that several startling realizations had come upon the disciples just before this. First, Peter had spoken for the disciples and openly affirmed his conviction that Jesus was indeed the Messiah.

"Who do people say that the Son of Man is?" [Jesus asked.] And they said, "Some say John the Baptist;

some, Elijah; and others, Jeremiah, or one of the prophets." He said to them, "But who do you say that I am?" And Simon Peter answered and said, "Thou art the Christ, the Son of the living God." And Jesus answered and said to him, "Blessed are you, Simon Barjona, because flesh and blood did not reveal this to you, but My Father who is in heaven" (Matt. 16:13-17).

Indeed, a great realization had come upon the disciples. But more than that, it was a great revelation. For God the Father Himself, not the flesh and blood of humanity, had revealed this truth of Jesus' messiahship.[1] And Peter's decisive, uncompromising affirmation of it marked a climactic step along the path God had prepared for him. For no sooner had he taken that step, than Christ granted him apostolic authority and privilege.

A TIME FOR RESPONSIBILITY

Jesus solemnly declared, "I also say to you that you are Peter, and upon this rock I will build My church; and the gates of Hades shall not overpower it. I will give you the keys of the kingdom of heaven; and whatever you shall bind on earth shall have been bound in heaven, and whatever you shall loose on earth shall have been loosed in heaven" (Matt. 16:18-19).

Obviously, some very important privileges have been granted by this declaration. For a more precise understanding of these privileges, however, we need to take a careful look at several aspects of the declaration. First, Jesus began with a very instructive play on words. "Peter" and "rock" are the two words played upon. And in the original language, these words sounded like this: "You are *petros* (Peter), and upon this *petra* (rock) I will build My church." The *petra* is evidently *petros*; Peter is one of the rocks upon which the church is founded.[2] And it is easy to see why he was called so now. He had just embraced a fundamental truth upon which the Christian faith is built. And to possess this foundational truth was a crucial requirement for foundational responsibility.

LAYING THE FOUNDATION

Not that Peter was the only one ever to be given this responsibility. For the Lord would give this privilege to others too, as Paul confirmed when he wrote that Christians are God's house, "having been built upon the foundation of the apostles and prophets, Christ Jesus Himself being the cornerstone" (Eph. 2:20). So other apostles and prophets were part of the foundation with Peter too. Nevertheless, Peter was singled out now for a couple of reasons. First, the timing of it underscored the relationship of the privilege to an uncompromising stand upon Jesus' messiahship. And second, Peter, more than the others, would assume a prominent place of leadership in the beginning of the church, in Acts 1—12.

The significance of his responsibility in the church was heightened by the assurance that the gates of hell would not overcome it. The "gates of hell" is a phrase used in the Old Testament to refer to death itself.[3] So Jesus was saying that even death will not overcome the assembly built upon the foundation of which Peter was a part. In other words, Peter was "getting in on the ground floor" of an eternal investment! And his contribution to it would have dividends forever. What a privilege and responsibility to be foundational to the only building that would never pass away.

But in what way would he be foundational? One way, of course, would be in his possession and proclamation of a foundational truth. But Jesus amplified Peter's foundational privilege in granting him the keys of the kingdom and the right of "binding and loosing."

The "keys of the kingdom" symbolized authority within the kingdom in the same way that the possession of house keys could picture authority over a house. The kingdom, in a sense, was thus likened to a house over which Christ was the Master. And as a homeowner might delegate responsibility to a servant and symbolize it by giving him the keys to the house, so Christ delegated responsibility to Peter and expressed it by giving him the keys of the kingdom.[4]

The right of "binding and loosing" clarifies this responsibility. "Binding and loosing" was a common way of expressing judgments on matters permitted ("loosed"), or matters forbidden ("bound"), or persons acquitted ("loosed") or persons condemned ("bound"). And in Peter's case, his judgments, Jesus told him, would reflect not the wisdom of man but the decisions of God. For what he bound or loosed would already have been done in heaven. So Peter was foundational not only in his possession of foundational truth, but in his right to exercise apostolic authority.

No doubt some of this authority was exercised in his first century apostolic responsibility. As an apostle, he would exercise discipline in the church (Matt. 18:18; Acts 5:1-11) and play a leading role in its beginning (Acts 1—12). And, of course, he exercised this authority also in the writing of his letters which are recognized as Scripture. But the privileges of his authority still have not been completely enjoyed. For Christ assured him that, in the future, he would also exercise that authority over the entire earth, when he and the other apostles share the rule of Christ in the messianic kingdom (Luke 22:24-30).

Peter must certainly have been elated over the privileges the Lord had given him. But I doubt if he were surprised about the kind of privileges they were. For when Peter thought of the Christ (or, in Hebrew, the Messiah), he thought primarily of a mighty ruler of the nation and the earth. He thought of one who possessed authority and, consequently, had authority to grant. And if Christ were to grant privileges to His followers, it would be natural, Peter would think, for that privilege to consist in a share of that messianic authority. A king he had recognized; a king's reward he had received.

A SECOND REVELATION

Peter had indeed realized a great truth when he had recognized Jesus as the Christ, the Ruler of the earth. But that recognition by itself was not enough. He needed also to receive a second truth. So "from that time Jesus Christ began to show His disciples that He must go to Jerusalem, and suffer many things from the elders and chief priests and scribes, and be killed, and be raised up on the third day" (Matt. 16:21). But because Peter (and the others) did not understand the resurrection, he really perceived only this: The Christ would suffer and die (Mark 9:9-10; Luke 18:31-34). This truth, however, Peter would not readily accept.

For him, the Christ was the mighty Ruler. And in this conception, he shared the ideas of his fellow countrymen. Few thought of suffering and death when they thought of the Christ. They thought of glorious rule under the mighty Leader of Israel. No wonder Jesus forbade Peter to proclaim Him as the Christ to the multitudes (Matt. 16:20). The crowds cherished the same half-truth as Peter and would hastily have tried to elevate Him to the throne. Before Peter and the others could proclaim Jesus as the Christ to rule, they needed to understand He was also the Savior who would die.

RESISTANCE AND REBUKE

Nevertheless, Peter stubbornly resisted. How could the glorious King of all the earth suffer and die? Peter would not hear of it. Furthermore, he was determined not to allow it. Scripture tells us that he even took Jesus aside and began to rebuke Him for considering so dishonorable a path (Matt. 16:22). The glorious rule Peter gladly accepted; the path of sacrifice he angrily rejected.

But Jesus recognized his prideful attitude as directly from Satan and against the purposes of God. Therefore, "He turned and said to Peter, 'Get behind Me, Satan! You are a stumbling block to Me; for you are not setting your mind on God's interests, but man's' " (Matt. 16:23).

TRUTH AND CONSEQUENCES

If Peter were to follow Christ and not Satan, he would have to accept this second great truth: Jesus was not only a mighty King but also a suffering Savior. But more importantly, Peter would have to accept the consequences of that truth, too. For as certainly as Christ's rule would bring to His followers a share of His reign, so His sufferings would bring to them a share of His sorrows. And, in fact, not only the disciples but all who would follow Him faithfully would have to be willing to share the pain of His rejection as well as the privilege of His rule.

As King, Christ offered a king's reward. And Peter gladly received it. As a suffering Savior, Christ offered a path of sacrifice and self-denial. And Peter must be willing to accept that, too. For in no uncertain terms, the Lord Jesus challenged the disciples to follow that path. Having rebuked Peter for his resistance to self-denial and suffering, Jesus turned to all the disciples and solemnly assured them that to follow Him would bring precisely what Peter rejected.

"If anyone wishes to come after Me, let him deny himself, and take up his cross, and follow Me. For whoever wishes to save his life shall lose it; but whoever loses his life for My sake shall find it. For what will a man be profited, if he gains the whole world, and forfeits his [life]? Or what will a man give in exchange for his [life]?

For the Son of Man is going to come in the glory of His Father with His angels, and WILL THEN RECOMPENSE EVERY MAN ACCORDING TO HIS DEEDS" (Matt. 16:24-27).

SHOULDER THE CROSS

Occasionally, someone experiencing a misfortune or difficulty in his life will comfort himself with the words, "Well, everyone has his cross to bear, and I suppose this is mine." While it is true that nearly everyone must contend with misfortune, not everyone bears the cross in the way Jesus meant when He challenged His disciples to deny themselves, take up crosses, and follow Him.

In the Roman world, the one carrying his cross was on his way to death with the executioner's block upon his shoulder.[5] This was the cross of which Jesus spoke. And if to imitate Him meant his followers would bear crosses behind Him, then it must also signify that Jesus would bear a cross in front of them. He had just told His disciples He would die. Now He told them how. And in the same breath, He called them to follow Him to that death by crucifixion.

Could Jesus be asking the disciples to be crucified alongside Him? Was He really asking them to imitate His death in this way? The answer is yes and no. No, because we learn from Luke's quotation of this challenge that Christ said His followers must take up the cross not once but daily (Luke 9:23). And if Christ had meant a literal execution, they could have taken up the cross but once.

But, yes, He was asking them to imitate His death in their lives on this daily basis. In His death (as in His life), He denied Himself His own privileges so that He might bring life to others. He asked the disciples in following Him, therefore, to deny themselves, too. That, of course, included a denial of their desire to sin. But it also included a denial of certain things not sinful at all in themselves.

For He called them to set aside their own ambitions and purposes. He asked that their lives might count not for themselves but for Him. In other words, He called them not merely to die for Him, but more difficult perhaps, to live for Him.

On the other hand, if His death were really their example, He called them to set no limits on their self-sacrifice, for He did not. And this could ultimately mean a literal death in their service for Him. History tells us that it meant just that for many of them. So their daily crosses would indeed one day be wooden crosses of death.

CROSSES AND WEDDING RINGS

For the most part, however, bearing the cross behind their Master meant a daily imitation of His death. Or from a broader perspective, it simply meant identifying with Him completely and accepting all the consequences—as a wife, for example, will identify with her husband and accept the consequences, too. She will experience not only the joys but also the sorrows of her husband. When he is honored with great financial privilege, she shares his wealth. When he struggles to provide the bare necessities of life, she shares his poverty. Similarly, the Lord Jesus was now asking His disciples to share not only in the wealth of His future reign but also in the poverty of His present rejection. If self-denial and suffering were a part of His life, it would have to be a part of their lives, too.

DOUBLE OR NOTHING

Jesus plainly assured them that the stakes were high on their decision to share His rejection. "Whoever wishes to save his life shall lose it; but whoever loses his life for My sake shall find it." The preservation of true life was at stake. The one who attempted to enhance and preserve a life in this world would ultimately lose that life. If he devoted his life entirely to acquiring honor and position in the present age, he would not have prepared for the age to come. His labors may have had a present reward but not a lasting one. Thus when the Lord returns, the life of temporal gain would be lost.

But the one who lived for Christ and His kingdom would ultimately gain his life. He would seem to many to be losing his life now, for he would not set his heart upon position and honor in the present age, but on approval in the age to come. But though his labors may have little present reward, they would certainly have a lasting one. For when the Lord returns, the life this disciple supposedly lost would be gained forever. It was not what this man had, but who he was that mattered most. And he had been a faithful follower of Christ.

A reasonable man, it seems, could only choose living for Christ. "For what will a man be profited," Jesus went on to say, "if he gains the whole world, and forfeits his [life]?" (Matt. 16:26) If a man's life consists in the ownership even of the entire world, that life is still destined to end. Either his own death or the return of Christ will conclude it. For when Christ returns to the earth, the title deed of this planet becomes His once again. So the life consisting in the honor of worldly possessions must certainly vanish.

Then what is left? If one has been wholly devoted to personal riches, and his relationship to God has dwindled to nothing, only the shell of the person he could have been is left. The shell has been filled with temporal pleasures and riches for himself, and when these end, the heart of his life ends too. What can he give for all the lost opportunities which might have given him riches forever? He may indeed have entered a personal relationship with Christ as the disciples had, and therefore be in heaven for eternity. But he has missed the great potential inherent in that relationship.

This possibility should not surprise us, though. The missed potential is a tragic reality in other important relationships, too. It frequently happens in marriage, for example. Two people, very much in love, enter an exciting life together. The days are too short for their time alone. A lifetime is not enough to give themselves to one another. But then ingratitude and apathy slip in. Soon the richness of the relationship is lost. He is filled with his personal ambitions. She is occupied with the children. One morning they wake up, the children are gone to college, the business supplies more money than is ever needed, but there is emptiness between them. The great potential has not been experienced. The couple may take significant steps to renew their love, but what can they give now in exchange for the years of missed opportunity?

It happens in our relationship to one another; it can happen in our relationship to Christ. And it is so regrettable in either case. For "what will a man give in exchange for his [life]?" One cannot buy back the missed opportunities to acquire "riches for heaven," when the market has closed. Each of us has but one life that can be lived faithfully for Christ through the trials of this life. And there will be no trials to endure for Him in heaven. So when that one life is over, so are the opportunities for faithfulness.

Yet our faithfulness establishes the quality of our relationship with Christ in the future. Hence Jesus adds, "For the Son of Man is going to come in the glory of His Father with His angels; and WILL THEN RECOMPENSE EVERY MAN ACCORDING TO HIS DEEDS" (Matt. 16:27). Both the faithful and not so faithful Christian will be recognized. To the one will go the reward of Christ's approval and its concrete expression in the designation of responsibility in

His kingdom. But to the other will come the disappointment of withheld approval and loss of reward. Of course, both will have the great reward of presence with Christ. But one will have cultivated a deeper appreciation and enjoyment of that presence. So even in this, the faithful Christian has the greater reward.

If the couple who lost the depth of their relationship through apathy and ingratitude were given the reward of a two-week vacation together, they could not enjoy it as much as a couple for whom a lifetime was still too short for their time together. Different qualities of marriage relationships develop; different qualities of Christward relationships develop too. But whatever development has taken place will be plainly evident when Christ returns to evaluate and reward His followers.

The Truth Comes Out

The prospect of this evaluation made an indelible impression on the lives of the apostles. Paul assured his Christian readers that "we must all appear before the judgment seat of Christ" (2 Cor. 5:10), not to see whether we will enter heaven or not, but to receive approval or disapproval from the Lord we serve. He encouraged his readers therefore not to judge one another, but to wait on the judgment of God. For not the praise of men but the praise of God mattered most. "Therefore do not go on passing judgment before the time," Paul wrote, "but wait until the Lord comes who will both bring to light the things hidden in the darkness and disclose the motives of men's hearts; and then each man's praise will come to him from God" (1 Cor. 4:5).

The apostle John encouraged his readers to set their focus on the return of Christ, too. "And now, little children, abide in Him, so that when He appears, we may have confidence and not shrink away from Him in shame at His coming" (1 John 2:28).

Of course, the apostles emphasized this prospect of approval or disapproval only because Christ had first done so. Now that they had entered a personal relationship with Christ through faith, nothing could compare in importance to His approval at His return. Had He not said that only the one who "loses his life for My sake shall [find] it"? Imagine what the disciples must have felt as they were confronted with all this truth. Peter and the others had realized that Jesus was the Christ, the One destined to rule the earth. And they were prepared to share His authority in the kingdom.

But now He informed them that the Christ would also suffer and die. And His followers must be prepared to share that humiliation. Not only this, but their willingness to do so would determine the ultimate worth and accomplishment of their lives. The value of all the world's goods could not purchase what loyal allegiance to Christ during persecution would gain.

THE REAL QUESTION

Of course, the most reasonable choice was to live for His future return and kingdom. Temporal reward could not compare to an eternal one. But the real question for them was not the reasonableness of the choice, but the truthfulness of it. If they were being asked to live for a future day, how could they be assured that this day would one day come? If they were being asked to eternally stake their lives on the word of Christ, what assurance did they have that His word was worthy of their trust?

A REASON TO BELIEVE

The mountain of splendor was intended to give them that assurance. And one way it would do so was by fulfilling a prophecy of Christ. For with fears and doubts burning in the minds of the disciples, Jesus uttered a startling proclamation. "Truly I say to you," He announced, "there are some of those who are standing here who shall not taste death until they see the Son of Man coming in His kingdom" (Matt. 16:28).

Although some have puzzled over what seeing "the Son of Man coming in His kingdom" meant, the event which Jesus predicted was precisely the mountain of splendor.[6] Peter himself who heard the prediction and saw the event tells us so. When he saw that miraculous scene on the mountain, he knew he had seen "the power and coming of our Lord Jesus Christ" (2 Pet. 1:16-18). In other words, Peter saw Christ's prediction fulfilled.

And the timing of this fulfillment followed a long standing precedent. For in the Old Testament, when a prophet challenged the people to return to God, he encouraged and warned them in light of the consequences of God's future kingdom. And to prove that he spoke truthfully of the future, the prophet would make predictions of a soon-to-happen event to assure his audience he was a true prophet.

Jesus also had done this. He had prophetically challenged His followers in light of His future kingdom. And then He predicted a soon-to-happen event to assure them of His trustworthiness. For if He could be trusted about this event in the near future, then it would be reasonable to trust Him about the kingdom in the far future, and accept the challenge based upon it. So when the mountain of splendor fulfilled His prediction, it assured the disciples that He was a true and trustworthy Prophet. The fulfillment of His prophecy is recorded as follows:

> And six days later Jesus took with Him Peter and James and John his brother, and brought them up to a high mountain by themselves.[7] [2]And He was transfigured before them; and His face shone like the sun, and His garments became as white as light. [3]And behold, Moses and Elijah appeared to

them, talking with Him. ⁴And Peter answered and said to Jesus, "Lord, it is good for us to be here; if You wish, I will make three tabernacles here, one for You, and one for Moses, and one for Elijah." ⁵While he was still speaking, behold, a bright cloud overshadowed them; and behold, a voice out of the cloud, saying, "This is My beloved Son, with whom I am well-pleased; hear Him!" ⁶And when the disciples heard this, they fell on their faces and were much afraid. And Jesus came to them and touched them and said, "Arise, and do not be afraid." And lifting up their eyes, they saw no one, except Jesus Himself alone (Matt. 17:1-8).

THE ORIGINAL V.I.P.'S

Thus did the mountain of splendor fulfill the prophecy and assure the disciples that Christ was indeed to be trusted. It also encouraged them to embrace Christ's challenge for a second reason. For when Christ was transformed, two great heroes of the past miraculously appeared and conversed with Him. To fully understand how their presence lended further assurance to the disciples requires a brief journey into their status in the Old Testament.

Moses was one of these heroes, and certainly no man was more famous in the nation's history than he. Raised in the court of a king, exiled to the fields and flocks of Midian, chosen by God to challenge the Egyptians and command the people of Israel, he was perhaps the strongest leader in Old Testament history. He was like a king in his authority, a prophet in his message, and a priest in his service to God for the people.

But more than these honored responsibilities, he was the mediator of the Ten Commandments and other laws in the national constitution prescribed by God for His people Israel. And so significant was he in its establishment that it was thereafter called the covenant of Moses. Even in the New Testament, it was called the Law of

Moses. And when referring to the entire Old Testament, although it was customary to designate it as "the Law and the Prophets," so identified were Moses and the Law that it was sufficient simply to call the Old Testament "Moses and the Prophets."[8] Moses was indeed a prominent figure.

Nevertheless, he was scarcely greater than the other hero of the past who talked with Christ. For Elijah was as qualified as any to stand beside the famous receiver of the Law. Nine centuries earlier, he had fought valiantly against the nation's idolatry with ringing words of judgment and astonishing miracles of prophecy and healing (1 Kings 17—19; 2 Kings 1—2). "There is no more dramatic figure in all biblical history than Elijah," wrote one scholar, "from the moment when he appears abruptly upon the scene announcing to Ahab in short, stunning words the coming years of drought and famine to the last act when he is rapt away into the heavens in a chariot of fire with horses of fire. The prophet was the incarnation of zeal for the Lord."[9]

Every true prophet of God should have been this way, of course. When the people would abandon the Lord, the prophets were raised up to call them back to God and His Law. But at the head of the long line of prophets faithful to the Law, Elijah was considered the most zealous and preeminent. Consequently, he and Moses shared a complimentary relationship to the Law. Whereas Moses was its human giver, Elijah was its guardian. And as Moses came to represent the Law, so Elijah came to represent the prophets. When we remember that "the Law and the Prophets" was a title for the entire Old Testament, we must conclude that Moses and Elijah could, by themselves, represent the heart of the Old Testament.

It is no wonder that they were considered to be the counterparts of one another.[10] But their complimentary relationship to the Law and their representation of the Old Testament are not the only reasons for this. They are also considered counterparts of one another because the patterns of their lives correspond in a remarkable way.

TAPESTRY FOR TWO

For example, both were men of the country rather than the city. Moses, for the better part of eighty years, lived in the pastures of Midian or the desert of the wilderness. Elijah was born in the obscure village of Tishbah, settled in the rolling hills and woodlands of Gilead, and never lived in the population centers of the day. And he, like Moses, spent an important part of his life in the solitude of the wilderness.

Perhaps more significant in the pattern, both initiated the two great periods of miracles in Old Testament history. Although some mistakenly believe that miracles occurred with a consistent frequency in the Old Testament, for the most part, they were confined to two time periods—a cluster of miracles began during the ministries of both Moses and Elijah and concluded in the lifetimes of each of their successors.

The conclusion of their lives continued the similarity of the pattern, for both of their lives ended in a mysterious way. In the case of Moses, God commanded him to ascend Mt. Nebo and gaze at the promised land. Then, quite astonishingly, God issued the command for him to die upon that mountain too, even though he was in the peak of health (Deut. 34:5, 7). Thus, he did not die an ordinary death, but one in obedience to the word of the Lord (Deut. 34:5).

The conclusion of Elijah's life was even more unusual, for it ended not in death but in flight! He had been walking along the Jordan speaking to Elisha of his departure when, suddenly, a chariot of fire and horses of fire came between them, and Elijah was caught up to heaven in a whirlwind (2 Kings 2:11).

The comparison does not end here, however. A further correspondence crystallizes after their deaths. Both of them had trained apprentices whose work strikingly paralleled and completed what they had begun. Moses had miraculously parted the Red Sea to lead the nation from Egypt; his successor, Joshua, miraculously parted the Jordan to lead the nation into the promised land. Elijah performed miracles of sustenance and restoration of life; his successor, Elisha, also performed miracles of sustenance and restoration of life.[11]

And quite significantly, just as Joshua crossed the Jordan after the death of Moses (Josh. 3), so Elisha miraculously crossed the Jordan in imitation of Elijah's miraculous crossing just before this (2 Kings 2:8, 14). It is as if the Scriptures are saying, "Look! Elijah was like Moses. Like Moses, he miraculously crossed the waters, and like Moses' successor, his successor began his work by miraculously crossing the Jordan."

Moses and Elijah were recognized as counterparts to one another because of their complimentary relationship to the Law, life in the wilderness, clusters of miracles, remarkable departures from this life, and the similarity of their successors' works.

In fact, it is difficult not to remember the pattern itself as one which, through God's special leading, marked out the two great servants of God who represented the Law and the Prophets.

But if the pattern marked out their lives so noticeably, it is only reasonable that its occurrence in the life of another man would mark him out also as a servant of the same caliber as they. In other words, not only do Moses and Elijah in their persons represent the Law and the Prophets, but by their life-patterns they may have alerted us to the kind of man through whom God would work in the future.

Now at last we can see why these two heroes of the past appeared with Christ.

ENDORSEMENT BY ASSOCIATION

Who else could have given the disciples more assurance that Jesus was truly the Messiah the Old Testament had foretold? The very men who represented the Law and the Prophets stood beside Him as confirmation of His claim. It would be as if an Englishman in America claimed to be the prime minister's son. One might be more convinced of his claim if one saw him in friendly association with the British ambassadors. How reassuring it was to the disciples that Christ stood between the representatives of the Law and the Prophets.

TAPESTRY FOR THREE

Then how much more assuring that He even shared the pattern which so noticeably emerged from their lives. As Moses and Elijah had known the solitude of the wilderness, so had Christ known the wilderness of conflict. And as Moses and Elijah had begun the two periods of miracles in the Old Testament, so had Christ begun the third and greatest period of miracles in the New Testament. Then as Moses' death and Elijah's departure were both strikingly unusual and surrounded by an aura of mystery, so Christ's death was to be different from anyone else's and mysteriously surrounded by a blackened sky, an earthquake, and strange events upon the earth. But His death was like the departures of Moses and Elijah in a more particular way too. Like Moses' death, Christ's death occurred while He was in the peak of health and in obedience to the will of God. Then as Elijah miraculously was caught up into heaven, so would Christ be raised miraculously from this planet.

Finally, whereas Moses and Elijah had successors who fulfilled their work and reproduced some of their miracles, so the disciples of Christ carried on His work and completed the third era of miracles. However, it is a notable contrast that Christ not only had similar successors, but He was also Himself the successor to the work begun by John the Baptist. When we realize that John the Baptist was a prophet who had come in the spirit of Elijah (Luke 1:17), then we must conclude that Christ, by analogy, was his Elisha. And like the successors to Moses and Elijah, Christ also began His career in the Jordan waters.

So the only way in which Christ departed from the pattern of Moses and Elijah is that He was also a successor Himself who crossed the Jordan and completed the work of His predecessor. But this one departure suggests that although Christ was fully in harmony with the men who represented the Law and the prophets of old, He was also their successor who will fulfill the Old Testament they represented.

It is difficult to know how much of this comparison the disciples grasped, as they squinted at the brightness of the scene. Probably very little. But as they later reflected upon Jesus' association with the two heroes of the past, what encouragement it must have brought them. For as the pattern of Jesus' life crystallized in their minds as that shared by Moses and Elijah, the disciples would have recognized God's identifying hand upon His life. The same God who mysteriously worked through Elijah and Moses was now working in a similar manner through His Son. God's hand was indeed upon Him. The timid disciples need not fear they were following an imposter.

So the mountain of splendor brought assurance to the disciples not only by confirming Jesus a true Prophet, but also by bringing Him into a fascinating association with Moses and Elijah. Nevertheless, it also encouraged them to embrace the words of Christ for a third reason. For it pictured the very kingdom the disciples would share. Remember that in the prophetic proclamation the event is described as "the Son of Man coming in His kingdom." But how could the transformation on the mountain fulfill this prophecy? Is it possible that the prophecy was not really fulfilled, and, therefore, the word of Christ is not to be trusted? "After all," it may be objected, "Jesus has not actually returned, and it's been many years since the disciples' deaths."

A MINIATURE PRODUCTION

It is true that the second coming did not occur in the disciples' lifetime. Nevertheless, I am convinced that they *saw* it. And I am convinced because I believe the mountain of splendor was like a prophetic vision which patterned the entire event.

Notice first of all, that Christ's appearance on the mountain of splendor strikingly resembled John's description of His appearance at His return. In the book of Revelation, the brightness of His exaltation is described like this: "His head and His hair were white like white wool, like snow; and His eyes were like a flame of fire; and His feet were like burnished bronze, when it has been caused to glow in a furnace" (Rev. 1:14-15). So when Christ returns, He will appear as He did in the radiant splendor.

Remember, secondly, that He was upon a mountain, and the Old Testament foretold that the Christ would descend upon a mountain at His return. "In that day His feet will stand on the Mount of Olives, which is in front of Jerusalem on the east" (Zech. 14:4).

Also, of course, when Christ returns, He will descend to His people. And Peter, James, and John could represent those to whom Christ would return. But He will return not only to His people, but *with* His people. And Moses and Elijah serve as perfect representatives of the kind of people with whom He will return.

For Moses died and went to be with the Lord. And he could represent all believers who died in Christ and will return with Him. But Elijah was miraculously received into heaven without tasting death. And he could well represent all believers who are alive at Christ's return and are caught up to meet Christ without tasting death, and then return with Him (1 Thess. 4:13-18).

So the prophecy by Christ was fulfilled. The mountain of splendor was a picture in miniature of His return. When the disciples recognized it as such, they could give themselves unreservedly to Christ in this age because they had seen a preview of the coming age. And thus the transfiguration encouraged the disciples, not only by confirming that Christ was a true Prophet, and by associating Him with Moses and Elijah, but also by foreshadowing the future reality for which He asked them to live and die.

The Glory Before the Grind

It is easy to see the psychology behind this preview. Imagine, for example, that a very mediocre football team is about to play the national champions. A thunderous roar greets the favored team when they enter the stadium. As the fearful visitors take the field, they see why their opponents are four touchdown favorites. They are larger, stronger, faster, and almost swaggering in their confidence. The underdogs would give anything to win. But how intimidated they feel by the awesome team they face.

Then imagine a "transfiguration scene." As the underdogs take the field, they see a vision before them more real than anything they had ever seen before. They see themselves sweat-streaked and dirty but wildly cheering. In the vision, the scoreboard reads visitors, 7; national champs, 6. Imagine what encouragement this would give them. With new energy and confidence, they would take the field and play their hearts out until they had won. They would know that their effort and sacrifice would not be in vain.[12]

And that is exactly what the disciples knew when they understood the meaning of the mountain of splendor. Their effort and sacrifice would not be in vain.

The Main Point

Of course, I would be the first to admit that this meaning did not dawn upon the disciples for quite some time. But to be certain they understood the main point, God the Father thundered forth a statement which became the fourth and final confirmation of His Son's trustworthiness. "Behold, a bright cloud overshadowed them; and behold, a voice out of the cloud, saying, 'This is My beloved Son, with whom I am well-pleased; hear Him!' " (Matt. 17:5)

The radiant cloud was the awesome, visible presence of the invisible God. As Peter fell silent before it, the voice of God the Father spoke. Do you remember hearing some of these words before? Except for the last two words, they were identical to the highly significant words spoken at the baptism. God the Father was once again placing His firm endorsement upon His Son. "This is My Son," identified Jesus as the Messianic King: "Beloved Son" identified Him as the beloved Son, like Isaac, who will give Himself in willing sacrifice. "With whom I am well-pleased" identified Him as the Servant-Priest of Isaiah.

But what about the additional words "hear Him"? Do they have a special meaning, too? In the first place, they do not mean simply to listen. The command to hear is really the command to obey. The old English word "hearken" translates it better. "Hearken to His words," "be obedient to Him"—is the meaning of the last phrase.

In the light of the technical nature of the other phrases,

we might expect this one to contain a technical meaning also. The prophecy of Deuteronomy 18:15 confirms our expectation. In this prophecy, Moses wrote, "The LORD your God will raise up for you a prophet like me from among you, from your countrymen, you shall [*hear him*]" (itals. added). More and more Israelites began to look for this prophet who would be like Moses in his greatness. We catch a glimpse of their anticipation when John the Baptist emerged as a mighty leader. The people wondered if he might be the Christ, Elijah, or—notice it well—"the prophet" (John 1:19-21). It was the prophet of Deuteronomy 18:15 that they were expecting.

So the people of Israel were indeed familiar with this prophecy. Doubtlessly, they knew each word by heart. And would it not be natural to think of it just now? Christ had spoken like a prophet. Now His prophecy had come to pass. Slowly, the conclusion would begin to dawn upon the disciples that Jesus was not only the foretold King, Priest, and Son, but He was also *the* foretold Prophet, in Deuteronomy 18:15. Then to remove any lingering doubts about that conclusion, the Father commanded obedience to His Son in the very words of that prophecy. There was every reason now to obey.

VIEWING THE VIEWERS

But what was the response of those who saw the event? In order to fully appreciate their response, we need to understand who were privileged to see it. Jesus had said that only some of the disciples with Him would see this event. And Peter, James, and John were the ones chosen. The choice is not surprising, however. These men were frequently alone with Christ. They, along with Andrew, sought special instruction about the second coming (Mark 13:3-4). They alone accompanied Him when He raised to life a young girl (Mark 5:37). And perhaps most significantly, they alone were asked to accompany Him through His struggle in Gethsemane shortly before He was crucified (Mark 14:33). Is it possible that those who would see His suffering most intimately needed also to see His glory most plainly? Perhaps so.

And maybe these three needed to see His glory most plainly because they would also be asked to intimately share that suffering in their service for Him. James was executed by Herod in A.D. 44. Peter was crucified upside down, during Nero's reign. And John faithfully followed Christ throughout his long life, bearing up under persecution and exile until, when an old man, he died in Ephesus.

But that was all future. On the mountain, they were still in the learning process. And they resembled three stooges more than three saints. Luke tells us they were sleeping when Christ first became a splendrous light (Luke 9:32). But perhaps this can be explained. When these same three men fell asleep in Gethsemane, Luke adds that it was because of their sorrow (Luke 22:45). They were escaping their sorrow by their sleep. Perhaps here too they slept because they were discouraged over their Master's words a week before. They were in a state of depression over the prospect of sharing His suffering. No wonder they needed a glimpse of His glory.

A RESPONSE OF CONFUSION

Peter evidently did not know what to think of all this, but simply blurted out in his excitement, "Lord, it is good for us to be here; if You wish, I will make three tabernacles here, one for You, and one for Moses, and one for Elijah."

His outburst did not reflect much insight, to say the least. Nevertheless, his words do indicate he had heard bits of the conversation between Jesus, Moses, and Elijah. For Luke tells us they had been speaking of the "departure" Christ was going to accomplish (Luke 9:31). Departure is simply a soft word for death. However, the word for "departure" quite interestingly is "exodus." Luke has recorded a very instructive play on words when he recorded their speaking of Christ's death as an exodus. For just as the exodus under Moses delivered the people from the bondage of Egypt, so did the exodus of Christ's death deliver His people from the bondage of sin.

But Peter evidently did not understand that it was the exodus of Christ's death that was being discussed. He simply heard them speaking of an exodus. And, naturally, the exodus he would recall was the exodus of the nation under Moses. Then I think we must assume Peter remembered that God's care for His people after the exodus was commemorated in the annual Festival of Tabernacles. For no sooner did Peter hear "exodus" than he blurted out the suggestion to build three of the tabernacles used in that celebration.

But, of course, Peter spoke too soon. The exodus of which Jesus spoke would not be celebrated until after His death. Whether aware of it or not, Peter was again resisting the suffering before the glory. But before he could finish his hasty outburst, the Father interrupted with the commanding proclamation of His Son.

A RESPONSE OF WISDOM

The Scripture says that the frightening radiance of God's presence and His thunderous voice of almighty authority stunned the spellbound disciples. "They fell on their faces and were much afraid. And Jesus came to them and touched them, and said, 'Arise, and do not be afraid.' And lifting up their eyes, they saw no one, except Jesus Himself alone" (Matt. 17:6-8).

Notice well the conclusion to the spectacular scene, "They saw no one, except Jesus Himself alone." That response was exactly what the event was intended to bring—a focus on Jesus alone. The disciples had been asked not only to rule with Christ, but also to suffer with Him. But to sustain them in their suffering, Christ had set before them His own example and His future kingdom. And as we have noted, when it came right down to it, He had asked them to stake their lives on His word about that kingdom.

But He had also shown His word to be eminently trustworthy. The mountain of splendor had confirmed Him a true Prophet, brought Him into association with Moses and Elijah, foreshadowed the reality He asked them to live for, and occasioned the authenticating voice of God the Father Himself. Now it was left to the disciples to see Him and Him alone as the goal to which they would run in the course of their lives.

A RESPONSE TO FOLLOW

Surely many of us are much like these disciples. We have realized, as they did, that a great many privileges and benefits came to us when we recognized that Jesus is the Christ. Forgiveness, new life, a new family, and a host of other things belong to us because we belong to Him.

But then, like the disciples, we come to a crucial point in our lives where we are confronted with the truth that to follow Christ faithfully means not only to receive His gifts but also to share His suffering. And then we wonder if it is worth it. Is the price too high? Is the prize too small? Is the kingdom only a myth?

Peter answered a resounding no to all these doubts. And he did so because he understood the full significance of the transfiguration: "For we did not follow cleverly devised tales when we made known to you the power and coming of our Lord Jesus Christ," he wrote, "but we were eyewitnesses of His majesty. For when He received honor and glory from God the Father, such an utterance as this was made to him by the Majestic Glory, 'This is My beloved Son with whom I am well-pleased'—and we ourselves heard this utterance made from heaven when we were with Him on the holy mountain.

"And so we have the prophetic word made more sure, to which *you* do well to pay attention as to a lamp shining in a dark place, until the day dawns and the morning star arises in your hearts" (2 Pet. 1:16-19, itals. added).

So Christ, through Peter, would set before us, too, His own example and kingdom. Like the disciples, we are to set our hearts on God's eternal kingdom and not a temporary one of our own. And we also are to see Christ and Christ alone as the goal to which we will run in the course of our lives.

5

THE HILL OF SACRIFICE

Some say that Adam died there, and there lieth; and
that Jesus in this place where death had reigned there
also set up the trophy. For He went forth bearing the
cross as a trophy over the tyranny of death: and as
conquerors do, so He bare upon His shoulders the
symbol of victory.

John Chrysostom, fourth century A.D.,
John, Homily LXXXV.

Jesus was not reluctant to leave the mountain of splendor.
But perhaps He should have been. For only a valley of
opposition awaited Him. No sooner did He leave the
mountain, for example, than He confronted a demon-
possessed boy, faithless disciples, and a populace that
resisted Him (Matt. 17:14-21). Furthermore, within a year,
that resistance grew to violent rejection. And that rejection, in turn, led to His death.

The amazing thing is that Jesus could already foresee
this entire sequence of events. But still He left the mountain. Willingly, without reluctance. "Resolutely," in fact,
"[He] set His face to go to Jerusalem" (Luke 9:51). Yet it
would ultimately mean His death, for there He would be
crucified. He had descended the mountain of splendor
that He might ascend the hill of sacrifice.

But how could this happen? Was it a tragic misfortune,
or an accident of history? No, the ascent up that hill was
the purpose of His life. He had said so Himself. He had
come, He said, not "to be served, but to serve, and to give
His life a ransom for many" (Mark 10:45). Evidently, the

climax of His service was His sacrifice. Although He served others much in His life, He would serve them more by His death. It was certainly no tragic accident of history. Neither was it simply the end of His mortal life. It was much more the goal of His life. It was not the end of the story, but the theme of the story.

THE SONG BEGINS

The Scripture gives it this place of central importance in countless ways, for His death is a primary theme of the entire Bible. Think first of the Old Testament. In these ancient scrolls, His death was both foreshadowed and foretold. It was foreshadowed, for example, from the very beginning, by aspects of animal sacrifice. For instance, when the guilt of Adam and Eve made them ashamed of their nakedness, God clothed them with animal skins (Gen. 3). And to supply these skins for covering, one must assume, of course, that animals were slain, So the shame of nakedness was covered by the death of innocent animals.

If we listen closely to this story, we can hear the first soft sounds of what becomes a major theme in the symphony of Old Testament revelation—guilt is covered through sacrifice. And, consequently, the approach to God is through sacrifice, because guilt separates a person from Him.

This theme is further developed in the next recorded event, after the clothing of Adam and Eve, for we read of their sons bringing gifts to God. Cain brought part of his harvest, but Abel brought an animal sacrifice (Gen. 4). And although we are not told why, only the animal sacrifice was accepted by God. Perhaps God intended us to see that sacrifice is not merely one way of approach to God; it is the only way.

But the theme of sacrifice is more fully developed in

Genesis. One does not read much further until he comes to the incredible command given Abraham to sacrifice Isaac upon Mount Moriah (Gen. 22). Numbed by the prospect of his loss, but gathering strength from his conviction that God could raise his son from the dead, Abraham obediently ascended his hill of sacrifice. However, as he was about to plunge the knife into Isaac, God prevented him. Isaac would not die. And instead of Isaac's death there would be the death of a ram God had provided in his place.

The test was over. But Abraham had learned a very important lesson. God is the One who provides the right sacrifice. In fact, the lesson was written so indelibly in his mind that "Abraham called the name of that place The Lord Will Provide" (Gen. 22:14a). And not only Abraham but also his descendants remembered this lesson. For the Scripture says there arose from this event for centuries the saying that "In the mount of the Lord it will be provided" (Gen. 22:14b). God would indeed provide the proper sacrifice upon the mount some day.

THE MELODY ENRICHED

But He would also reveal even more of the meaning of sacrifice. And He did so next in the story of the Passover (Exod. 12). Moses had declared that the tenth plague of death would come upon the land of Egypt. Every firstborn son in the land would be slain. Yet the people of Israel could be spared by a lamb of sacrifice. The blood of this lamb would have to be placed upon the doorposts. And when the Lord would see this blood He promised to "pass over" that house and not allow the angel of death to enter. So the Passover lamb would save the sons from death.

If we learned from this event only that sacrifice can deliver from death, we would have seen merely an interesting variation of something we already knew. For we

91

have just observed that Isaac's life was spared by the sacrifice of a ram in his place. But there is more to be learned from the Passover than this. If we read the story more carefully, we discover that the lamb to be slain must be "an unblemished male a year old" (Exod. 12:5). Only a mature, unblemished male lamb would protect from the angel of death. So the sacrifice had important qualifications of purity.

But we also can learn at least one more thing. After this protection from the tenth plague of death, the people of Israel made their exodus from Egypt and commenced their journey to the new land God had promised them.

Thus the Passover sacrifice is one which marks a departure from an old way of life and the beginning of a new way of life. The specially chosen lamb of purity not only saved from death but also commenced new life. These are additional developments in the truth about sacrifice the Old Testament has unfolded.

THE ORCHESTRA JOINS

Nevertheless, the greatest enrichment of the theme of sacrifice has not been mentioned. Shortly after the Passover, God gave Moses upon Mount Sinai the national constitution for Israel. And in this constitution was specified an elaborate system of sacrifice which we could not begin to detail. But it is instructive to observe that every national feast, every act of worship, every approach to God on every day of the year was possible only through sacrifice.

There was sacrifice for guilt and sin, and sacrifice for thanks and service. There was sacrifice to commemorate God's acts in the past and consecrate His work in the present. In the morning worship, there was sacrifice. In the evening worship, there was sacrifice. The centrality of sacrifice could not have been plainer. The ritual was no incidental option for the believer in God in the Old Testament. It was a fundamental requirement of his life. So the importance of sacrifice comes through loud and clear in the elaborate system of Old Testament worship.

ECHOES OF THE SONG

Thus the meaning of sacrifice has been progressively given by all of the Old Testament revelation. Think of it. From Adam and Eve, we learned that sacrifice covers the guilt of sin. From Abel, we learned that it is not merely one way to God, but the exclusive way to God. From Abraham, we discovered that the proper sacrifice will ultimately be provided by God. From the Passover, we saw that the sacrifice of a mature, unblemished male lamb could save from death and commence new life. And, finally, from the centrality of sacrifice in the national life of Israel we grasped the importance of sacrifice in the life of worship.

How remarkably all of this prepares us to understand the death of Christ. When this theme in the symphony of Old Testament revelation reaches a resounding climax in His death, the reality of the shadows has come. He is the mature, unblemished male provided by God as our covering for guilt. And exclusively through Him is there relationship to God and the beginning of new life. The ancient scrolls did indeed foreshadow the death of Christ in their development of the theme of sacrifice.

THE WORDS OF THE SONG

But the Old Testament did more than foreshadow His death. It also explicitly foretold it. Many aspects of His death are described, and three times we are even told that He would be pierced through. This seems all the more interest   when we realize that death by crucifixion was unknown when these descriptions were given.

Nevertheless, in Psalm 22 we read a description of His

death in the first person which includes the words, "They pierced My hands and My feet"[1] (Psalm 22:16). In Isaiah 53, we discover a fascinating passage which mentions this piercing, too. The passage in its context describes His death as follows.

> Surely our griefs He Himself bore,
> and our sorrows He carried;
> yet we ourselves esteemed Him stricken,
> smitten of God, and afflicted.
> *But he was pierced through for our transgressions,*
> He was crushed for our iniquities;
> the chastening for our well-being fell upon Him,
> and by His scourging we are healed.
> All of us like sheep have gone astray,
> each of us has turned to his own way;
> but the Lord has caused the iniquity of us all to fall on Him.
> (Isa. 53:4-6, itals. added)

Finally, in Zechariah 12:10, we are told again that Christ would be pierced. Yet Psalm 22 was written 1,000 years before His death; Isaiah, 700 years; Zechariah, 500 years. These predictions first strike us as being miraculous prophecies, and they are. But they also tell us that the death of Christ was of central importance even in the Old Testament.

The Singer Comes

It is no wonder that His death was given this importance in the New Testament, too. The gospels, for example, variously devote between twenty and forty percent of their record to the last week of Jesus' life. Then after the four gospels, the book of Acts essentially becomes a record of the world's responses to the message of Jesus' death and resurrection.

After Acts, one turns to the epistles—the letters written by the apostles to individuals or groups who had responded to that message. But even in these letters, the death of Christ is central. For the letters are basically an application of Christian truth to practical situations. And the essence of Christian truth, particularly as Paul unfolded it in Romans, is simply a development of all the implications of Christ's death and resurrection.

A SONG FOREVER

One might think that after he had read these epistles, he would have finished all the emphasis on the death of Christ. After all, only the book of Revelation would be left, and that book speaks of the future. But it also speaks—in fact, it sings—of the One who holds the future. And the words of the song which echo through the choruses of heaven praise the death of Christ, the Lamb of God. "Worthy is the Lamb that was slain to receive power and riches and wisdom and might and honor and glory and blessing" (Rev. 5:12). Even in the book of Revelation the hill of sacrifice has the center of attention.

So let it be said again. His death was no tragic accident of history. It was not simply the end of His life but the goal of His life. It was not the end of the story but the theme of the story. From the slain animals of Genesis which clothed Adam and Eve to the slain Lamb of Revelation who receives honor and praise, the sacrifice of Christ is portrayed. If we wish to grasp the meaning of Christ's life and the theme of the Scriptures, we must look with understanding at this important image in the miraculous mirror, the hill of sacrifice.

OF GOOD AND EVIL

A conspiracy of evil men, under the mysterious hand of God, brought this sacrifice. Threatened by His goodness, envious of His following, and fearful of His growing authority, the religious leaders maliciously plotted His death. Many of the religious officials joined in the intrigue. Many more gave their silent consent. At last, they made contact with a man on the inside of their Rival's activities. And this follower of Jesus agreed to set Him up for arrest in a place where no crowd resistance could spoil the plan.

The place was Gethsemane where Jesus had gone for solitude. And there in its silence, He wrestled with His Father's will. Not because He was afraid of physical death. Had that been all He faced, there would have been no struggle. But He agonized because He dreaded the spiritual death that would come from bearing the penalty of others' sins.

It is true that many of His followers embraced the death of martyrdom more easily than He accepted the death of sacrifice. But it is only because the former could not compare in pain to the latter. Yet there in Gethsemane, He submitted to the will of the Father. He had done so at the Jordan's waters of judgment, at the subsequent wilderness of conflict, and, indeed, throughout His life. He would not turn aside now.

A Night for Conspiracy

Even as Judas came to identify Him that night for an untroubled arrest in Gethsemane, Jesus did not flinch. In fact, the strength of His presence completely stunned the soldiers who came to seize Him. But the armed soldiers gathered their courage and took the unarmed civilian to those who had plotted against Him. The religious officials then questioned Him harshly. Jesus answered honestly that He was the Christ sent by God. This only infuriated them more and intensified their clamor for His death. For that, however, they would have to wait until morning.

But all through the night, the men who held Him in custody subjected Him to humiliation. They beat Him, spit upon Him, and mocked His claim to be Christ. And when the morning came, they handed Him over to the civil authorities who had the right of execution. It was almost the undoing of their scheme though. For Pilate was the civil authority over their region, and he was neither naive nor imperceptive. He knew little about religion but much about men. And he could see it was not out of a desire for justice but out of envy that the execution was desired (Matt. 27:18).

THE DAY OF INJUSTICE

Nevertheless, he did not wish to stand in the way of the mob. So when he heard that the accused was from Galilee, outside his own jurisdiction, he jumped at the chance to rid himself of his responsibility. Immediately, he sent Jesus to Herod Antipas, the official who ruled Galilee. Herod refused to take the case, however, and Pilate was left with the decision. Actually, it should not have been a difficult one to make. The innocence of the accused was clear. But the cries for His death were loud. So although Pilate had sought His release in the beginning, he gave in to the relentless pressure in the end.

Jesus would be crucified. Already He had been scourged. The lethal whip with pieces of rock and metal imbedded in its thongs had torn His back to shreds. But that was not enough to satisfy those drunk with hatred. Jesus must be crucified. So up the hill of sacrifice they pushed Him. The cross block was on His back, and a wreath of thorns was thrust upon His head. And all around Him was the crowd howling, barking, and growling like animals.

It seemed more like a jungle than a city. The conspirators were like leopards confident of their prey, and their followers were like buzzards bloodthirsty for death. The soldiers seemed like lumbering, insensitive bulls, dragging their load behind them. And the gathering crowd of mockers and cynics seemed like a pack of mongrel dogs which yelped and growled at the disturbance.

Among all these animals only one man could be found. And quite astonishingly, He was the one about to die. Yet His manliness, self-composure, and dignity were never more apparent than as He persevered up the hill, surrounded by the inhuman creatures intent on His death. He did not yell or curse back; He did not struggle to get away. As it had been prophesied of Him long before, He set His face "like a flint rock" and resolutely plodded onward (Isa. 50:7).

EXECUTION

At last, they came to the place of execution, nailed Him to the cross, and hoisted Him off the ground to die. The physical pain was unimaginably intense. The gospels do not describe it, however. But, of course, their readers did not need an instructive description. Many had likely seen crucifixion personally. Those who had not seen had undoubtedly heard of it. They knew of the procedure. First the hands of the victim were either bound or nailed to the crossbeams. He was then hoisted up and affixed to the upright, and then the feet were nailed. His body weight would have torn his hands from the wood, except that he sat astride a wooden block in the center of the upright. This also prevented a quick death by suffocation from an inability to raise up oneself for breath. So the wooden seat did not ease the pain but prolonged it. The intensity of it is difficult for us to imagine. But those of the first century knew it well.

For those of the twentieth century, however, one scholar wrote the following description.

"A death by crucifixion seems to include all that pain and death can have of the horrible and ghastly—

dizziness, cramp, thirst, starvation, sleeplessness, traumatic fever, tetanus, shame, publicity of shame, long continuance of torment, horror of anticipation, mortification of intended wounds—all intensified just up to the point at which they can be endured at all, but all stopping just short of the point which would give to the sufferer the relief of unconsciousness.

"The unnatural position made every movement painful; the lacerated veins and crushed tendons throbbed with incessant anguish; the wounds, inflamed by exposure, gradually gangrened; the arteries—especially at the head and stomach—became swollen and oppressed with surcharged blood, and while each variety of misery went on gradually increasing, there was added to them the intolerable pang of a burning and raging thirst, and all these physical complications caused an internal excitement and anxiety, which made the prospect of death itself—of death, the unknown enemy, at whose approach man usually shudders most—bear the aspect of a delicious and exquisite release."[2]

One thing is clear. The first century executions were not like the modern ones, for they did not seek a quick, painless death nor the preservation of any measure of dignity for the criminal. On the contrary, they sought an agonizing torture which completely humiliated him. And it is important that we understand this, for it helps us realize the agony of Christ's death.

THE SEVEN MAGIC THREADS

It is even more important, however, to perceive the *meaning* of His death. For it will help us very little to understand the pain of the cross, if we do not also grasp its purpose. And perhaps there is no better way to gain that understanding than by standing very close to the cross and listening to the last words of Christ's mortal life. He spoke seven times, and each time He illuminated the meaning of His death.

A THREAD OF SILVER

Scarcely had the nails pierced His hands when Christ spoke the first words from the cross. "Father, forgive them," He gasped, "for they do not know what they are doing" (Luke 23:34). Perhaps the most amazing thing about this is simply that it really happened. A Man of unquestionable innocence really asked mercy for those who cruelly put Him to death. It would be inaccurate to call this a miracle, but surely it is almost as amazing as one.

However, one thing is puzzling about these words—at least to some readers. It is the reason He gave for requesting the Father's mercy, "Because they do not know what they are doing." Does this mean that ignorance excuses or lessens the gravity of sin? The answer is yes and no.

Yes, ignorance does lessen the gravity of sin. The Scriptures teach that. For example, at the conclusion of a parable, Christ drew the lesson that the "slave who knew his master's will and did not get ready or act in accord with his will, shall receive many lashes, but the one who did not know it, and committed deeds worthy of a flogging, will receive but few" (Luke 12:47-48). But, no, ignorance does not excuse the responsibility for sin. For in this very parable, the ignorant slave still received lashes. And Christ still asked forgiveness for those who killed Him in ignorance. He would not have done this had there been no sin to forgive. So ignorance lessens the responsibility for sin, but it does not excuse it. That is not a lax view of sin but a strict one. For wrong done in ignorance is still sin in need of punishment or forgiveness.

This means, therefore, that the Lord Jesus could have rightly asked for the punishment of those who killed Him.

But, of course, He did not. And it was not only an astonishing surprise but an invaluable example. For it was the climactic example of an attitude He had expressed throughout His life. It was an attitude of compassion, not only for the homeless and the hungry, which He shared with many before and after Him, but also of compassion for the guilty. And few, before or after Him, shared that. The guilty received condemnation but not compassion. Yet for those burdened with the guilt of sin, the compassion of Jesus was greatest.[3]

Even when the guilt was from sin against Him. Many have compassion on the poor, and some have compassion on the guilty, but few have compassion on those guilty from sin directed against them. These first words thus become not only the crowning example of His compassion but also the climactic demonstration of a difficult assignment He had requested of His followers. For at the outset of His public life, He had issued a demanding challenge to them. "Love your enemies and pray for those who persecute you in order that you may be sons of your Father who is in heaven; for He causes His sun to rise on the evil and the good, and sends rain on the righteous and the unrighteous" (Matt. 5:44-45). Now He demonstrated the attitude He had told them must characterize their relationships.

As difficult as it seems to imitate this example, it is at least not impossible. Stephen is proof of that. He was the first Christian to die because of his service for Christ. And as his murderers stoned him to death, the book of Acts records that "falling on his knees, he cried out with a loud voice, 'Lord, do not hold this sin against them!' " (Acts 7:60) Shortly before this, however, Stephen saw a miraculous vision of the Lord Jesus in heaven (Acts 7:56). Possibly that is how Stephen received strength to imitate Him. And it may be that others will receive strength that way, too. If not by a miraculous vision, then at least by looking to Christ and then listening with understanding at these first words from the cross.

A Gift for All

Perhaps the most fundamental lesson from these words, however, has yet to be mentioned. It is implied by a simple observation. For we may observe that forgiveness is asked not merely for those who do not deserve it, but also for those who never receive it. This can happen because forgiveness is a two-way street. One must offer it; another must receive it. So the Father could grant the forgiveness requested by His Son, and yet those for whom Christ prayed could refuse to receive it. And it seems that is what many of them did.

Particularly when we realize for whom He prayed. Some have thought it was only for the soldiers, since they were the only ones who acted in ignorance. But the apostle Peter informs us that the entire nation acted in ignorance, too. When he addressed several thousand of his countrymen after the crucifixion, he said very plainly, "And now, brethren, I know that you acted in ignorance, just as your rulers did also" (Acts 3:17). So Christ prayed not only for the soldiers when He prayed for those acting in ignorance; He also asked forgiveness for the people and rulers.

Yet the majority of them never received it. It was offered but not taken. The spotlight of this first saying thus comes to rest on the provision of forgiveness, even for those who never receive it. At least the forgiveness is provided. And that may be the most fundamental lesson one may learn from this first saying from the cross—not merely that we must offer forgiveness to others, but that God has offered forgiveness to all, even to those who reject it.

102

But, thankfully, the cross brought a forgiveness that was received by some. And Christ's second saying from the cross guaranteed just that to one desperate man who was being crucified beside Him. Along with another criminal being executed, he had initially shouted insults and ridicule at Christ (Luke 23:39-41).

Then he came to his senses. He realized who he was, and what he deserved. And he also realized who Jesus was, and what He could do. With a changed attitude, he spoke out of his pain to the Lord. "Jesus, remember me when You come in Your kingdom."

"Truly I say to you," Jesus firmly told him, "today you shall be with Me in paradise" (Luke 23:42-43).

When the thief asked to be remembered, he was obviously not asking Jesus simply to erect a memorial to him in the coming kingdom. He was asking that he might share in that kingdom. It was a use of language similar to the frequent request, "O Lord, hear my prayer." One is not asking simply that his prayer be heard, but that it also be answered after it is heard.

In a similar fashion, the thief was not asking simply that Christ would remember him, but that Christ would deliver him when he was remembered. But although he asked only for a place in the kingdom in a future day, he was promised a place in paradise that very day.

The forgiveness which would bring a place in the kingdom had been offered to many. But the thief was one of the few who had the faith to receive it. He then learned from experience that the mercy offered would be granted, if requested. And what faith he showed by his request.

For he could see that Jesus was about to die. And it was a criminal's death at that. He could also see that nearly all of Jesus' followers had abandoned Him. Yet in spite of all this, he also perceived that Jesus was the One with power and authority in the coming Kingdom of God. So of the King in authority, he asked mercy. And it certainly reflected his faith.

But it also further revealed the compassion of Christ. He was concerned not only for man in general but for individuals in particular—even the desperate, dying individual beside Him. It has been said that Christ would have died with His hands outstretched no matter what the form of execution. For although He was in a dreadful condition Himself, He was still concerned to answer the request of the thief beside Him.

And when He did so, He answered him not merely in words of sympathy but in words of authority. To have answered only with sympathy might have eased the burden, but it would not have answered the request. But Christ answered him with the authority of a king extending His favor to a subject. He did not say, "Perhaps I can help," or "Maybe the Father will help," but *"Truly* I say to you, today you shall be with Me in paradise" (itals. added).

Although Christ's crucifixion had resulted from the rejection of that very authority, He still sovereignly exercised it upon the cross. It was a demonstration of His royal dignity at its best. For it was set against the background of man at his worst. So His second saying from the cross not only guaranteed mercy to the one who asked, but, in doing so, also revealed the compassion and authority of a king.

A THREAD OF VELVET

His next words illuminate His selflessness even more. Beneath the cross, four soldiers paid little attention to Him. The only thing they found of value in His death were His clothes they gambled for. But also beneath the cross was the disciple John. He had returned to the vicinity after first fleeing with the others when Jesus was arrested.

Several women who were followers of Christ were also there. His mother was one of them. And it is necessary to remind ourselves again that this really happened. On a specific day in history, the mother of Jesus stood motionless in grief before her son she loved and cared for.

No doubt she longed to ease His pain, to cover His body, to bring Him water, or wipe His brow. Perhaps she even stepped toward Him to do that. But, of course, the soldiers would have prevented it. She could only stand in helpless sorrow before her dying son.

But then He turned His eyes upon her. Perhaps the corners of His lips turned slightly upward, and His eyes squinted softly. His face softened as if to smile. "Woman," He said gently, "behold, your son!" And He may have motioned with a slight movement of His head to John.

Then He said to John, "Behold, your mother!" (John 19:26-27) "From that hour," Scripture records, "the disciple took her into his own household."

It is difficult to think of anything that could reveal Jesus' thoughtfulness more than this. The pain, the sleeplessness, rejection by the people, mockery of the crowd, abandonment by His friends—all would have left even the best of men bitter, or at least self-concerned, but Jesus' concern was for others.

And if He were not overwhelmed by the pain of the cross, we would surely expect Him to be absorbed with its importance. For He considered it the purpose of His life and the hope of the world. But neither the pain nor the importance of the cross so gripped Him that He could not turn in compassion to His mother. And whereas the thief had requested His mercy, Jesus extended it to His mother without being asked.

His last words to her are at least an eloquent illustration of obedience to the fifth commandment: "Honor your father and your mother" (Exod. 20:12). He surely did just that when He provided for her welfare after His death. Mary's husband Joseph had evidently died some years before. And without the help of another family member, a widow in the ancient world was frequently reduced to poverty. With Jesus gone, that might have happened to Mary. But He saw to it that she was secure in the home of John.

A PUZZLE AND A CLUE

But why did He not entrust her to one of His four brothers?[4] They were seemingly next in line for the responsibility of their mother. And they were likely as capable of financial support as John.

John anticipated this question, I believe. And he has already answered it by informing us that these brothers had not yet recognized Jesus as the Christ sent by God (John 7:3-5). But, of course, John had recognized this long before. And he had come to know and love Christ deeply. That is why Mary was entrusted to him. She would find more spiritual nourishment with him than with her sons. For both she and John could share their mutual love for Christ. So Jesus was concerned not only for Mary's physical welfare, but for her spiritual welfare, too.

And how complimentary their relationship would be. No one was ever more aware of Christ's humanity than Mary. For she had given Him birth and watched Him grow in her home. Yet no one was ever more aware of Christ's deity than John. For of all the writers of the New Testament, John drew most attention to Christ's deity. It is likely true that the deeper two people know Christ, the deeper will be their relationship to one another. If so, what a foundation for relationship John and Mary thus shared in their complimentary perspectives of Christ.

Once in the past, Jesus had been told that His mother

and brothers were seeking to speak to Him. But He turned to the one who had informed Him and said, "Who is My mother and who are My brothers?" Then Jesus stretched out His hand toward His disciples and proclaimed, "Behold, My mother and My brothers! For whoever shall do the will of My Father who is in heaven, he is My brother and sister and mother" (Matt. 12:48-50). So in a very real sense Christ did entrust Mary to one of His brothers, for John was one of His many brothers in the family of God.

One last question remains. Why did He choose the hour of His death to give Mary a new son and John a new mother? He could have done it before the cross, since He had long foreseen His death. Or He could have done it after His death, since He also foresaw His resurrection.

It is entirely possible, of course, that this timing is not significant. Neither Matthew, Mark, nor Luke even recorded this third saying. On the other hand, perhaps God enlightened John to see something in the unusual timing which the others did not see. And perhaps that is why he, unlike the others, recorded these words in the first place.

SECOND SIGHT

But what did John see? Once again I believe John has anticipated our question and has answered it earlier in his gospel. For throughout his gospel, John has given a second and deeper meaning to words, sentences, events, and persons. For example, when John recorded Jesus telling Nicodemus he must be born again, the word for "again" also means "from above" (John 3:3). And both meanings clarify the result of faith. It is both a second birth ("again"), and also one which originates from God ("from above").

He records the use of a word in a double sense again when he cites Jesus affirming, "And I, if I be lifted up from the earth, will draw all men to Myself" (John 12:32). The word for "lifted up" can mean "lifted up for crucifixion" or "lifted up in exaltation." Yet both these meanings describe His death. For His crucifixion apparently humiliated Him, and yet because it was a voluntary act of love, it greatly exalted Him.

Sometimes sentences bear a second and deeper meaning, too. Caiaphas, one of the conspirators against Jesus, uttered such a sentence without even realizing it. As high priest of the nation, he presided over a council which convened to discuss the problems raised by Jesus' ascending popularity. Many expressed their fear that the growing allegiance to Jesus would bring a crushing reprisal from Rome and severe restrictions upon their nation (John 11:47-48). And although the solution of violence lurked silently beneath the surface of their thoughts, none ventured to suggest it as an answer to their problems.

Caiaphas was not so timid, however. He branded their reluctance as a mark of their weakness and foolishness. "You know nothing at all," he scornfully told them, "nor do you take into account that it is expedient for you that one man should die for the people, and that the whole nation should not perish" (John 11:49-50). The end justifies the means, he said in effect. And thus he justified a crime against one for the good of the many, at least so he said. It was more likely the good of their own skins they had in mind.

But notice the second and deeper meaning of his words. In a very real sense, Christ did die for the nation—not to maintain the *status quo* Caiaphas desired but to bring forgiveness and life to those who believed. John perceived this deeper meaning and proceeded to say that Caiaphas did not say this "on his own initiative; but being high priest that year, he prophesied that Jesus was going to die for the nation; and not for the nation only, but that He might also gather together into one the children of God who are scattered abroad" (John 11:51-52). So not only words but sentences too can bear a second meaning in John.

Nevertheless, the most famous of that which bears a deeper meaning in John are the miracles he records. John calls them signs because they signify important truths. Very often he tells us precisely what truth it is. For instance, Jesus fed 5,000 men along with their wives and children. That was the sign (6:1-15). Then Jesus proclaimed, "I am the Bread of Life" (6:35). That was the truth being signified.

Or the order may be reversed. Jesus declared, "I am the Light of the world." That is the truth. Then He miraculously gave sight to a blind man. That was the sign attesting the truth (9:5-7). Or again, Jesus proclaimed the truth, "I am the Resurrection and the Life." Then as a sign attesting that truth, He raised Lazarus from the dead (John 11:25, 43-44).

Evidently John enjoyed presenting us with words, sentences, and events which carried a second meaning. Sometimes the meaning is merely additional, as with the birth "again" and "from above." Other times the meaning is ironically deeper, as with "lifted up" in crucifixion and exaltation, or with Caiaphas' evil intention expressing a sublime truth. Finally, with the signs, one might call the second meaning the symbolic meaning because the sign pictures a greater truth.

This symbolic meaning is, I believe, the second meaning which certain characters can bear. Consider Barabbas, for example. He was a criminal awaiting execution. Yet because of a local custom, he was a candidate for freedom on the day of the Passover. For the custom brought the release of one criminal on this national holiday.

Yet on this day, Pilate also presented Jesus as another candidate for freedom. Jesus, by all rights, should have been released, and Barabbas executed. But the people cried out for the death of Jesus, and, consequently, Barabbas was set free. He left his prison cell because Christ would go to the cross. And thus he lived because Christ would die. Or as John described them, the innocent died in place of the guilty (John 18:38-40).

Who can overlook the symbolic significance of Barabbas? Every believer in Christ is represented by Barabbas. His name literally means "son of the father." And every true son of the Father gains his freedom from sin's prison cell of condemnation because as Christ died in place of Barabbas, so Christ died in his place, too (John 1:12; Gal. 3:26). He has believed the One proclaiming his freedom, and has taken the step of faith to leave his prison cell.

John obviously had a knack for recognizing the second meaning in things. And that is likely why he perceived in the third saying from the cross the significance of its unusual timing. For the time and place became significant when he regarded the event with representative meaning.

THE MEANING OF THE VELVET THREAD

As Barabbas was set free because Jesus was condemned, so John and Mary became a family because Jesus died. And that is the primary reason they can represent all believers who become family because Jesus died. As the prison cell of Barabbas pictured man's condition apart from Christ, so John's and Mary's place beneath the cross pictured the place where Christian family is experienced.

Perhaps the greatest hindrance to the experience of Christian family is pride. It creates divisions and prevents the unifying work of love. But standing beneath the cross, it is very difficult to cling to the pride of wealth, knowledge, or accomplishment. As one contemplates the death of Christ, he can scarcely think of anything but the need he shares with every man, and the need he acknowledges with every believer. That person is then prepared to listen

110

to the One upon the cross who tells him that those beside him are his family.

Christ's third saying from the cross is thus not only a fulfillment of the fifth commandment and a sign of his concern for Mary's spiritual welfare; it is also a direction to every believer seeking the place of Christian family. The place is beneath the cross of Christ.

A MYSTERIOUS DARKNESS

Jesus had claimed He was the Light of the world. His first three sayings are evidence of the claim. For against the dark background of the injustice against Him, His words are like three stars breaking through the darkness of night. Or perhaps they are more like the first rays of morning light which shimmer across the darkened earth and announce the light of the coming day.

But more light of any sort would be delayed. For not long after His words to John and Mary, the sky began to strangely darken. In a short time, midday became twilight and twilight became midnight, and a supernatural darkness had fallen upon them all. The crowd became quiet and began to disperse.

Something strange and fearful was happening. One could feel it all around him. But what was it? Some looked to the sky for an answer, and others to those around them. But then a horrible cry came from the central cross. "MY GOD, MY GOD," Jesus cried out, "WHY HAST THOU FORSAKEN ME?" (Matt. 27:46) And in this cry they had their answer.

The darkness Jesus had resisted had engulfed Him. Not the darkness of the sky but the darkness of sin. And the darkness of the sky had simply foreshadowed it.

Punishment for the sins of others was falling upon Christ. And the punishment for sin was separation from God first through spiritual death and secondly through physical death. Christ would soon taste the second but now experienced the first. And when He did, His cry of agony shot through the darkness like a thunderbolt.

A Thread of Black

"My God, My God," He cried out. It was a significant beginning to His plea. For every other time He had prayed to God, He had always addressed Him as Father. Only here, in all of Scripture, does He address Him with the less personal "God." But now He evidently regarded Himself not in a family relationship but in a judicial one. He saw Himself not as the eternal Son before His Father but as a man before God.[5]

For only as a man could He suffer man's punishment for sin. And when He did thus suffer, He experienced all the guilt and loneliness that sin can bring. That is why He then cried out, "Why hast Thou forsaken Me?" He had indeed been forsaken by the Father as punishment for the sins of others.

That is the meaning of the fourth saying from the cross. But not only do the words of this saying tell us its meaning, but the picture of the cross proclaims it too. Picture first the crown of thorns upon His head. From Genesis, we learn that the curse upon man brought thorns to the earth. "Cursed is the ground because of you," God told Adam. "In toil you shall eat of it all the days of your life. Both thorns and thistles it shall grow for you" (Gen. 3:17-18). But now these thorns which came from the curse were thrust upon Christ. And it is a vivid picture of the curse upon man thrust upon Christ.

Picture also the cross of wood. Those who hung upon it were regarded as under the curse of God. For in Old Testament times, a criminal was hung upon a wooden tree and designated under God's curse (Deut. 21:23). But in

New Testament times, the Roman cross became the tree of execution. And, consequently, he who hung upon it was also reckoned under the curse of God (Gal. 3:13). So not only the crown of thorns but also the cross of wood proclaimed that a curse had brought His cry of forsakenness.

Imagine also the humiliation of His nakedness. The soldiers lacked the decency to wait until His death to parcel out His clothes. So naked upon the cross He hung. This event, like the thorns, must likely be set against the background of Genesis. For it is recorded that the sin of Adam and Eve brought not only thorns from the earth but shame from their nakedness. Because of the sins of others, Christ's nakedness brings Him shame.

The gospels thus paint a cruel, stark picture of Christ forsaken on the cross. His cry reveals the forsakenness. But the picture of the cross illuminates the meaning why. The curse had been thrust upon Him like thorns upon His head. He was as accursed of God as a criminal hanging from a tree. And therefore He experienced the shame His nakedness depicted.

No wonder the apostles spoke so frequently of His death in our place. "Christ redeemed us from the curse of the Law, having become a curse for us" (Gal. 3:13). "He made Him who knew no sin to be sin on our behalf" (2 Cor. 5:21). "While we were yet sinners, Christ died for us" (Rom. 5:8). "For Christ also died for sins once for all, the just for the unjust" (1 Pet. 3:18). They spoke of this so often because it was foundational to their forgiveness.

Because Christ was punished, they need not be. For when He was punished, it was complete. He endured every consequence of sin. And the picture of the cross tries to capture those consequences. Of course the consequences were more horrible than the pictures can say. He suffered a pain more painful than thorns. He endured a curse more accursed than a criminal's. And He experienced a shame more shameful than nakedness. But still the pictures give us some insight into the suffering Christ experienced for us.

A Thread of Scarlet

Perhaps that is why John captures these consequences of sin in a statement which is also a picture. It is the fifth saying from the cross and simply recorded as, "I am thirsty" (John 19:28). Jesus gasped these words shortly after His cry of forsakenness. And no doubt one reason He did so was because of the suffocating thirst that crucifixion brought. So His words indeed remind us of the physical agony He experienced.

But possibly they mean something more. For remember it is John who recorded them. And it was he who saw a second and deeper meaning in the third saying from the cross. Perhaps he also perceived the second meaning Christ intended in these words, too.

But how does one discover this meaning? The first step is to learn what thirst means elsewhere in John. And then the second step is simply to see if that meaning found elsewhere is appropriate also in Christ's words from the cross.

Unraveling the Thread

Thankfully, John does not leave us without help. For on three occasions other than the cross, Jesus spoke of thirst. And on each of these occasions, it bore a symbolic meaning.

The first occasion was at a well outside the village of Sychar, when He spoke with a woman of Samaria (John 4:1-29). She had been married five times and was presently living unmarried with another man. She had evidently been trying to quench her thirst for life at the fountain of romance. And no doubt she imagined each new man in her life to be someone who would at last bring her

114

the companionship and love she desired.

But it had been like drinking salt water. The more desperately she drank, the more thirsty she became. She was a disillusioned, lonely woman when Christ saw her at the well.

He initiated the conversation with her by asking her for a drink. And she lowered her bucket to quench His thirst from the noonday heat. But then He spoke to her of a "living" water that would quench her thirst forever.

"If you knew the gift of God," Jesus said, "and who it is who says to you, 'Give Me a drink,' you would have asked Him, and He would have given you living water" (John 4:10). "Everyone who drinks of this water shall thirst again," He said, perhaps nodding toward the well," but whoever drinks of the water that I shall give him shall never thirst; but the water that I shall give him shall become in him a well of water springing up to eternal life" (John 4:13-14).

From these bits of their conversation, the meaning of thirst becomes clear. It is the absence of eternal life. And this we know because the water quenching the thirst is no less than the gift of God (v. 10) which is the water of eternal life (v. 14). So if one is yet thirsty, he must lack the gift of life that satisfies that thirst.

But this thirst also means that one lacks a relationship with God. For later Christ described eternal life as simply knowing God. "And this is eternal life," He prayed to the Father," that they may know Thee, the only true God, and Jesus Christ whom Thou hast sent" (John 17:3). So if eternal life is a relationship with God, then the absence of eternal life must mean the lack of this relationship. And that, consequently, is the meaning of thirst. He is thirsty in the desert of life who is separate from the refreshing waters of the Father.

On the second occasion Jesus spoke of thirst it evidently meant the same thing. On the day before this occasion, Jesus had miraculously made bread for over 5,000 people. The next day He spoke of another bread more important to seek; it was He Himself "the bread of life," whose nourishment lasted forever. In the midst of His remarks, He proclaimed, "I am the Bread of Life; he who comes to Me shall not hunger, and he who believes in Me shall never thirst" (John 6:35).

Notice that once again thirst is quenched by faith in Christ, and the one who thirsts lacks eternal life. For eternal life is precisely what faith in Christ brings to quench the thirst.

This leaves one last occasion to consider. At the conclusion of an annual religious festival called the Feast of Tabernacles, Jesus stood and cried out a message loud enough for all to hear: "If any man is thirsty, let him come to Me and drink. He who believes in Me, as the Scripture said, 'From his innermost being shall flow rivers of living water' " (John 7:37-38).

John added that the water of which Jesus spoke was the Holy Spirit who would indwell every believer after Christ ascended to the Father (John 7:39). But if the water specifically represents the gift of the Holy Spirit, then the thirst must more specifically represent the absence of God's presence. So generally thirst represents spiritual death and separation from God, but specifically the absence of God's life-giving Spirit within.

THE MEANING OF THE SCARLET THREAD

That is the symbolic meaning of "thirst" in its usage before the cross. And quite significantly that is also its meaning after the cross. If one cared to examine its usage in John's other long writing, the book of Revelation, he would discover that even in it, thirst bears the same symbolic meaning. Twice, in fact, the gift of eternal life is described as water offered to the thirsty (Rev. 21:6; 22:17).

And the only other mention of thirst likely refers to the spiritual thirst which the presence of God will completely satisfy in the future.

Now if both before and after the cross the meaning of thirst is symbolic in John, is it not likely symbolic at the cross as well? Would "I am thirsty" upon the lips of Christ not then mean that the Source of all life, the very One who offered the water of life to every believer, now thirsted because He lacked spiritual life?

The answer must likely be yes. And, in fact, Christ could offer to quench the thirst of others only because He Himself would one day thirst. John's recorded words of Christ, "I am thirsty," bear a symbolic meaning similar to Matthew's and Mark's, "MY GOD, MY GOD, WHY HAST THOU FORSAKEN ME?" That fourth saying tells us explicitly that Christ was forsaken so that believers need not be. John tells us symbolically that Christ has thirsted that our thirst might be quenched.

The same truth has been told in two ways. But there is one important difference to observe. John's expression draws attention to the guilty feelings from sin, whereas the other expression draws attention to the legal penalty of sin.

Normally sin, like crime, will bring both penalty and guilt. A criminal will likely suffer an objective legal penalty of, for example, a five-year imprisonment. But he will also likely suffer from the subjective feelings of guilt and loneliness while serving his sentence. Similarly, Christ suffered first the legal penalty of separation from the Father. His forsakenness tells us that. But also He suffered the personal guilt and shame that sin must bring. And His thirst upon the cross casts the spotlight on that. So Christ completely suffered both the legal and personal guilt of sin.

How wonderful for us that He did. First, because the believer now need not be punished. He need not suffer

117

the legal penalty of abandonment by God nor the personal penalty of agonizing thirst. So his conscience need not condemn him because Christ was completely condemned in his place.

But because Christ has so suffered, we also can know He understands how we feel. Frequently, one feels so guilty that he thinks that no one has ever felt as guilty as he. But that is wrong. For Christ knew not only the legal penalty of sin but the feelings of guilt as well. He knows the sickening displeasure over sin that one can feel.

And whether we can explain this or not, we feel we can draw near to someone who empathetically understands us. An incident in Dallas several years ago illustrates this truth. A young boy was in an accident which necessitated the amputation of one of his arms. He withdrew from his family and friends and refused to talk to anyone. He was literally wasting away in withdrawal from life.

A friend of mine went to the hospital and asked if he might visit with the young fellow. This friend was met with skepticism but was allowed to visit the boy. When he came to the room, he saw the youngster staring out the window. The boy turned to see his visitor, who also lacked an arm. The boy looked at him for a few moments in silence. Then he said angrily, "You don't know how I feel, you couldn't."

"No, friend, you're wrong," the man said, "I do know how you feel. I also have lived without an arm."

The young boy hesitated a moment longer in his anger. Then he broke into tears as he ran toward my friend and put his one good arm around him. It was the beginning of the lad's recovery, which began when he found someone who really understood him.

It may be true that few people can empathize with the depth of guilt one may feel. I doubt that is true. But even if it were, one thing is certain. The Lord Jesus can empathize more deeply than we know with the guilt and thirst anyone may feel. His experience of thirst in our place not only means forgiveness can be offered us. It also means that when we come to Him to receive it, we come to Someone who fully understands the feeling of our thirst.

A Thread of Light

Yet it was not because He experienced that thirst forever. One may have expected Him to do so. For He suffered in man's place, and man's penalty was separation from God forever. But because this Man was also God, His suffering was infinite in worth those hours upon the cross. So when that time was over, the thirst, darkness, and pain ended too. The work He had come to do had been done. Like a triumphant warrior, He cried out, "It is finished!" (John 19:30)

It was only one word in the Greek—*tetelestai*. It had always been a melodic word in its sound. Now it became a beautiful word in its meaning. The work of God for man was completed. The gift of life had been purchased. The sacrifice for sin was done.

Some readers have thought the Victor's cry a bit premature. They have pointed out that the full penalty for sin must include physical death. And since Jesus had not died physically, then technically the work was not done. They are right, of course, that the penalty of sin includes physical death. And technically, it does follow that His work would not be complete until His death.

But surely the most difficult part of the work was over, and its conclusion so certain that the victory could already be claimed. As a matter of fact, it was not uncommon for Jesus to proclaim something yet future as already having been accomplished when its occurrence was certain.

For example, in John 13:31, one learns that Judas had just left to contact the soldiers who would arrest Christ.

The arrest in turn would lead to the trials of Christ and eventually to His death. And because this death would demonstrate His love, it would glorify Him to the utmost degree. Thus Judas takes the first step along a path that leads to the glorification of Jesus. Technically, the glorification would not come until the day after Judas took the first step to it, but practically the glory of Christ in His death was assured when Judas took that first step. And consequently, after Judas left to meet the soldiers, the Lord Jesus could say, "*Now is* the Son of Man glorified" (itals. added).

One sees a similar pattern of thought in the victory cry from the cross. The physical death of Christ was yet future, but the conclusion of His work was assured. So He could confidently say, "It *is* finished!" (itals. added).

What an unexpected word it must have been that hour! Midst all the pain and sorrow came the golden sound of *tetelestai*. In a voice of joy and strength and relief, it rang out.

Most people know the satisfaction of completing a long and difficult task—the pleasure of the last page of work, of receiving the diploma, of swimming the final lap, of jogging the final mile. Multiply that feeling by a thousand times, and one may grasp the exhilaration that flooded the body of Christ when He glimpsed the completion of His lifework. It lasted only for a moment, of course. For that is all His body could stand. But what a joy it must have been.

And what confidence it was intended to bring us. For it assured us that no need remains to finish the work that He already finished. Since He completed the work of suffering for sin, no one else need do that. The gift of life was fully purchased. It need only be received through faith in the One who bought the gift and gives it freely.

A great work had certainly been accomplished. No wonder He proclaimed the fact so heartily. And no wonder He then could rest so peacefully. "He bowed His head," John writes, "and gave up His spirit (John 19:30).

AT LONG LAST REST

The expression "he bowed his head" is used elsewhere in the gospels to describe the laying of one's head down to rest (Matt. 8:20). "The Son of Man has nowhere to lay His head," Jesus had said using this phrase (Luke 9:58). But now that His work was over, He did have a place. Upon the wooden pillow of the cross, He laid His head and rested from His work.

A THREAD OF BLUE

And as He died, He uttered a prayer. "FATHER," He said, "INTO THY HANDS I COMMIT MY SPIRIT" (Luke 23:46). It is a remarkable conclusion to His death. For in this prayer, He demonstrated His unwavering confidence in His Father. And He did so at a time when every circumstance made such confidence appear foolish. His enemies had apparently triumphed. His friends had deserted Him. His suffering was not only intense but unjust. His emotional energy was spent. Yet still He entrusted His life to the Father. What an astonishing example of faith. So by His words, He showed not only the way to die but the way to live.

THE PATTERN OF THE SEVEN THREADS

In a sense, all the words from the cross show the same thing. The first saying, "Father, forgive them; for they do not know what they are doing" (Luke 23:34), is the supreme example of compassion for one's enemies.

Then the words to the thief reflected a royal dignity undaunted by the opinions of those around Him: "Truly I say to you, today you shall be with Me in paradise"

(23:43). What a pattern for anyone to note who always casts a fearful eye at the opinions of others. For God intends that we see His eye upon us and gain our identity and peace from His approval. That is what Jesus did. And, consequently, when all around Him doubted and ridiculed Him, He acted no less a king.

Next Christ's words to His mother and John reflect a love that transcends even the most difficult circumstances (John 19:26-27). That is surely a love worth remembering when the slightest problem will close one's heart to others.

The terrible crisis of forsakenness and thirst came next from the cross (Matt. 27:46; John 19:28). Of course, no one other than Christ could suffer in the place of others like He. But one may still seek to imitate the love which led Him to do it. It was a love for which no sacrifice was too great if it might bring life to others.

The ringing words of His work accomplished then rang out, "It is finished" (John 19:30). They furnish a goal toward which all may strive who serve the Father. No one would finish a work just like Christ's, but all can finish a work that He gives. The apostle Paul expressed that sense of accomplishment when, near the end of his life, he wrote, "I have fought the good fight, I have finished the course, I have kept the faith" (2 Tim. 4:7). Everyone faithfully serving in the place God has placed him will be able to say the same thing.

Finally, the prayer before His death is a model of faith in desperate circumstances (Luke 23:46). So every saying from the cross is a lesson to follow, a sparkling facet of our fourth image in the miraculous mirror of Christ's life.

THE DEATH OF DEATHS

But every saying is not only a model to follow but a message to receive. And we have already observed the special message of each one. The first offered forgiveness to all. The second encouraged its reception by some. The third promised family at the foot of the cross. The fourth and fifth showed us the foundation for new life, Christ's suffering for the guilty. The sixth declaration assured us that the work for our forgiveness was completed. And the final saying reflected the confidence that we may also have in God to care for us. How remarkable are the words from the cross that they can bring not only so lofty a model but also so needful a message.

The Magical Portrait

The seven sayings are like seven magical threads which, woven together, display an astonishingly beautiful portrait of God's love. The Scripture says very simply, "God demonstrates His own love toward us, in that while we were yet sinners, Christ died for us" (Rom. 5:8). One may understand some facets of that love in the words of Christ from the cross.

But perhaps one may build upon that understanding by further contemplating the depth of His love against the background of His rejection. One sensitive person once said it something like this: His brow which had only wrinkled in concern for others, now dripped blood from thorns. His eyes of purity and compassion now looked upon inhuman men who mocked Him. His hands which had reached to help and comfort had nails pierced through them now. His feet which had walked hundreds of miles with the message of the kingdom were also nailed to the wood. And, finally, the heart which was more open and vulnerable than any other's could ever have been was now pierced through with a spear.

It is a vivid portrait of tough love, is it not? One sometimes reads, "Smile, God loves you." Does this not reflect a superficial understanding? Perhaps someone who truly grasped the love of the cross would write, "Cry . . . God loves you."

THOSE WHO MISSED THE PORTRAIT

Of course, not everyone responds to the cross in the same way. Some, I suppose, were not capable of recognizing it. Perhaps Herod was like that. Remember, he was one of the civil authorities who interrogated Christ. He was anxious to see Christ perform a miracle but not so ready to receive His teaching. And so to him, Christ said not a word (Luke 23:8-12).

Pontius Pilate was another who did not comprehend the love of Christ. He could see much, but he could not see that. He could see the innocence of Christ (John 19:6). And he could see the envy of His accusers (Matt. 27:18). But he gazed too much at the security of his position to look uncalculatingly at the love of Christ.

THOSE WHO LOVED THE PORTRAIT

On the other hand, some responded in quite a different manner. Perhaps the crucified thief who requested a place in the kingdom is a prime example. And what understanding he reflected in his request.

He evidently had perceived the deity of Christ, for he knew Him as One who had authority in the kingdom to come. This meant, of course, that he also believed in the reality of that future kingdom. He also realized that he was helpless to enter it in his own strength or by means of his own goodness. In fact, he explicitly told his bitter friend crucified with him that they both deserved their suffering, but Christ did not. "Do you not even fear God, since you are under the same sentence of condemnation? And we indeed justly, for we are receiving what we deserve for our deeds, but this man has done nothing wrong" (Luke 23:40-41).

Most important of all, the thief who had faith apparently understood that was all he needed. He understood that a place in the kingdom was a gift received through faith. And so by faith he did receive it. What remarkable insight the suffering thief possessed.

One might profitably ask what path led him to such insight. Perhaps some childhood instruction came back to him. Perhaps the conversation of some around him informed him. And, of course, Christ Himself, in all His magnetic presence, was right beside him. All of this may have contributed to his insight. But no doubt in part it was his own suffering which alerted him to the truths he needed.

The thief had learned what some never learn in their entire lives. Evidently, one must sometimes be brought to a place where Christ is all he has that he might discover that Christ is all he needs. And that much the thief had learned.

Others responded to the love of Christ but in a slightly different way. Nicodemus and Joseph of Arimathea were two of these. Both had long been believers in Christ, but both were afraid to admit it. They knew what might happen if they did. Consequently, Joseph had not talked personally with Christ at all. Nicodemus did little more. For although he did seek personal conversation with Christ once, he did so in the secrecy of the night.

Nevertheless, after the death of Christ, they both gathered up courage, came forth, and asked that they might prepare His body for proper burial. They no longer feared the consequences of publicly identifying with Christ. Perhaps they felt they should have done so long before. But no matter, they were certainly going to do it now. These secret disciples, as John calls them, were unwilling to be secret anymore.

Whereas the cross brought the thief his first taste of new life, it brought the secret disciples to public admission. But what did it bring those who had been faithful all along? If we remember John's experience, we will know. John had stood at the foot of the cross and entered a new family relationship with Mary. And there he represented all who would experience family beneath the cross. So even the faithful disciple had a deeper experience of family life when he contemplated the cross.

TWENTIETH-CENTURY ONLOOKERS

A wide range of responses were certainly brought forth from the cross. They varied all the way from the disinterest of Herod to the devotion of John. But although the centuries have come and gone, the kinds of people who respond have stayed the same.

Some today are like Herod, superficial and self-centered, seeking only the entertainment of a magician, but not the love of the cross. Some are like Pilate, wise and courageous by most standards, but not wise or courageous enough to face a hostile crowd and do what is right before Christ.

Others are like the thief. Just as desperate and just as undeserving. Yet they take the water of life without cost. And as surely as the kingdom shall come, they shall be in it.

A great many are no doubt like the secret disciples. They have believed in Christ and gratefully received the water of life. But they are not grateful enough to tell others they now belong to Christ. Nevertheless, they, like Nicodemus and Joseph, may gather their courage in response to the cross.

Finally many responders are like John and Mary; men and women who gain their true identity and true family from their relationship to Christ.

One thing is certain; if one responds like the thief, the secret disciples, or John, then one's confidence has been well placed. First, because one's trust is in the most trustworthy Person in the universe. One has confidence in the truth of One who claimed to be Truth itself. And second, because the Scripture offers miraculous attestation not only to all its message, but particularly to its message from the cross.

Most of the events around the cross had been predicted long ago in miraculous prophecy. Even each saying from the cross was predicted in one manner or another long before it was spoken.

The prophet Isaiah, for example, had foretold that the Christ would intercede for the guilty (Isa. 53:12). And that He did explicitly in the first saying from the cross, and implicitly in His assuring words to the thief.

Shortly after Christ was born, Simeon prophesied to Mary that the work of her son would pierce her heart with sorrow. And surely this was fulfilled as she stood beneath the cross and heard His words to her and John.

Perhaps one of the most remarkable prophecies came a thousand years before Christ's death, when David began Psalm 22 with, "My God, my God, why hast Thou forsaken me?" For he expressed the pain and agony of a man who is being crucified (Psalm 22:14-18). And, of course, the opening words of this psalm were echoed by Christ in the fourth saying from the cross, as He endured the experience that psalm described.

The prophecies do not end there, however. When Christ thirsted and was offered sour wine to drink, it was evidently a fulfillment of Psalm 69:21. In this psalm, as possibly in Psalm 22, David, through the Holy Spirit, could speak of events in his life which were prophetic of events in the life of Christ.

127

Of course, the meanings of the fourth and fifth sayings from the cross were prophesied in places other than Psalms 22 and 69. From Isaiah 52:13—53:12, for example, the meaning of Christ's death as being in the place of others is repeatedly emphasized.

Although the sixth saying is not expressly predicted, its meaning is nevertheless foretold. For the Old Testament, in many places, assured the world that the Christ would not turn aside until His work was done (for example, Isa. 50:4-9).

The seventh saying, on the other hand, found its precise expression hundreds of years before, in Psalm 31:5. And it occurred in the midst of the psalmist's experience of intense suffering, just like Christ's.

The seven sayings are indeed like magical threads—not only because of their lovely color but also because of their prophetic origin. And that prophetic origin was one very special way in which God attested their message.

But He also did so in another way. On the third day after they were spoken, He raised His Son to a miraculous new life. On that day in history, the greatest miracle of all attested the message from the cross. And it was an event seen by many as certainly as they had seen anything in their lives.

The Scriptures had predicted that, too (Isa. 53:10). And when it happened, history recorded it. Those who doubt it, doubt both divine Scripture and reliable history. And they also doubt the life of every disciple who was willing to live and die for its truth. For from that resurrection event came a movement spreading like wildfire across the Roman world with the message of the cross. And those who doubt must answer this question, what kind of match could have started such a fire—a deception, disillusioned disciples, or, as was claimed, the resurrected Christ with the message of the cross?

One is not indulging in wishful thinking as he contemplates this fourth image in the miraculous mirror of Christ's life.

6

THE PLAIN OF BATTLE

And darkness was removed, and the hosts of Mordor wailed, and terror took them, and they fled, and died, and the hoofs of wrath rode over them. And then all the host of Rohan burst into song, and they sang as they slew, for the joy of battle was on them. . . .

J. R. R. Tolkien, *The Lord of the Rings,*
Vol. 3, *The Return of the King*

The geographical importance of Palestine seems far out of proportion to its size. But thus it has always been. One reason is clear from a glance at a map. To the north lies the great Eurasian land mass; to the south lies the vast continent of Africa, and Palestine is the narrow land bridge between the two.

A closer look at an ancient road map would reveal that the international route between Eurasia and Africa had crossed this land for centuries. "Over it passed messengers, caravans, and countless military expeditions in every age."[1] This ancient route was known as the *Via Maris,* "the way to the sea," because travelers from Eurasia to Africa would eventually be led beside the Mediterranean shores along the way.

But before coming to the sea, travelers passed through many cities of the land's interior. For along this international highway the most ancient and important cities of the country had arisen. One of these was Megiddo, whose importance, like that of the land, seems far out of proportion to its size.

Nevertheless, an even closer look at the map will show the reason. For at Megiddo, the various branches of the *Via Maris* converge like the spokes of a wheel, and unite to form one chief route. It is no wonder that armies through the centuries have sought to command this crucial city, for the nation who held this primary junction controlled the only major route between Eurasia and Africa. The *Via Maris* and its branches, one scholar notes, "were always the great powers prime objective in their conquests of Palestine and Syria."[2] So Megiddo may have been small, but its military significance was great.

THE ARENA OF BATTLE

Nature herself seems to have anticipated this city's role in military history. For long before man ever set foot upon this land or traveled the *Via Maris*, nature carved out a valley of several hundred square miles beside the site of the future city of Megiddo. One can scarcely imagine a more natural battlefield. It stretched from Mt. Tabor on the east, to Mt. Carmel on the west, to Ibleam in the south.

In this vast plain, even the largest armies would have ample room for troup assembly, organization, and maneuvers. And the mountains around the plain could serve as excellent observation posts. It is like a colossal stadium, of which the mountains and hills are the stadium seats, and the valley below is the field of competition. So when the gladiators of the earth have battled for the *Via Maris*, they certainly have had an arena in which to do it.

This arena has been known throughout the ages as the valley of Jezreel. And if we had stood on its mountains from the beginning of history, we would have seen battle swords flashing across it in nearly every century.

From our observation post, we would have seen how the Egyptian Pharaoh Tuthmosis III defeated the Canaanite kings at the battle of Megiddo in 1468 B.C. On a rainy day in the twelfth century B.C., we would have watched Barak of Israel route the Canaanite charioteers, neutralized by the mire from the rain (Judg. 4:15; 5:1-4). A bit later in that century, we would have seen the Israelite Gideon defeat the highly mobile Bedouin marauders along the borders of the valley (Judg. 7).

But we would also have witnessed the death of King Saul in the eleventh century B.C. on Mt. Gilboa beside the valley (1 Sam. 31:8). And in Megiddo itself, we would have watched the fatal wounding of the Israelite king, Josiah, by an archer of Pharaoh Necho as he was marching to fight the Babylonians in 605 B.C. (2 Chron. 35:20-24). On and on the battles would have continued through the centuries even to the twentieth, when the British commander, Lord Allenby, fought the Turks at the Battle of Megiddo, in 1918.

THE GRAND FINALE

Nevertheless, all these battles pale into insignificance when compared to the greatest battle that will be fought there. For it is prophesied that on this plain, the last great battle of the world will be fought. But it will not be called the battle of Jezreel or even the battle of Megiddo. Although it is described in many places in the prophetic Scriptures, it takes its name from one particular reference in Revelation.

In Revelation 16:16, the battle preparations are being described. The evil kings of all the earth have been gathered together under the direction of demonic spirits for the final battle. And the gathering place of these kings is designated as the "mount of Megiddo."

In Hebrew, however, the word for mount is *har*; therefore, this place of battle is called Har-Magedon (Rev. 16:16). And it is from this rendering that the final battle draws its title: the Battle of Har-Magedon. Of course, for most people the two words have been joined into one. So the title of this last great conflict has come to be known simply as the Battle of Armageddon.

Thus in the ancient valley of Jezreel one last fierce struggle will take place. For centuries the warrior's blood has stained its soil, and its mountains have echoed the clash of swords and the shouts of battle in every age. But one last momentous time the battle cry will be heard in that valley. Across a field strewn with countless graves of swords, chariots, rifles, and metal, the most violent armies of the earth will march to war.

The demonic forces will first direct the hostility of these armies against one another. But that is only to draw them together for battle. Once they have gathered at Jezreel, the demonic forces will direct the hatred of the armies towards the returning King of the earth, the Lord Jesus Christ. Then the plain of Jezreel will be His battlefield.

PATIENCE AND WAITING

He has long anticipated that battle. After His resurrection He spent forty days on this planet with the disciples. He ate with them, taught them, encouraged them. At last, He informed them specifically of their future responsibilities in continuing the work He had begun. And He was quick to add that they would not do it alone. His presence and power would be with them in the person of the Holy Spirit. But the Holy Spirit would come to them only after He had ascended to the realm of the Father.

So after the forty days were concluded, He did indeed ascend to the Father, into a realm which transcends our own. He did not go simply to a higher place in our space-time dimension, but to a higher dimension itself—to a realm transcending space and time, into the very presence of God the Father. And just as He promised, He then

134

commissioned the Holy Spirit to the disciples to bind them together in a common Spirit and empower them for their service.

This does not mean, however, that the Lord Jesus was no longer active. He was, in fact, still directing His followers, but He was doing it through the Spirit. And, furthermore, He was continually praying for them to His Father.

But let us never forget that He was and *is* still waiting in eager anticipation of His last battle, the last titanic struggle on this planet as we know it, when "again the swords will clash and the soldiers fiercely rage." In many ways, there will never have been a battle like this one. Of course, its intensity and extent will distinguish it from any other. But so will its participants. For it will be the first time in history that the battle lines will be so sharply drawn between the forces of good and the forces of evil.

It will not be like much of modern wars where one side often seems as right as the other. Instead of black hats and white ones, they all seem to be grey. And what true man can swing his sword with the fullness of his strength when his conscience makes him doubt the cause for which he fights? Nevertheless, in this last battle, the side of the good and right will be clearly defined.

THE ULTIMATE CONFLICT

That is one reason, incidentally, why the Scripture designated the place of battle as beside the mount of Megiddo. Some have wondered why the battlefield is not designated simply as the plain of Jezreel or, as others have called it in the past, the Valley of Esdraelon. Why pinpoint the mount of Megiddo?

Perhaps because the author of Revelation was a skillful artist. And he was aware that the forces of good will proceed from another mount—Mt. Zion and Jerusalem (Isa.

59:20; Rom. 11:26). What better way is there to cast the spotlight on the nature of the two opposing forces than to display them both on prominent mountains in the land? On Mount Zion will be the warriors from heaven; on Mount Megiddo, the evil kings of all the earth. The former will be inspired by righteousness; the latter will be empowered by hatred and demons. On the mountain of good and the mountain of evil they will take their stand. And the winner of the conflict will rule the earth.

Of course, the prophets of God leave little doubt who the victors will be. The battle will be fierce; the casualties great; the destruction unequalled. But the warriors from heaven will triumph absolutely. And then, just as absolutely, the answer to the Lord's prayer will be given, for God's will shall truly be done on earth as it is in heaven. For when the mighty One from heaven comes, "The bow of war will be cut off. And He will speak peace to the nations; and His dominion will be from sea to sea, and from the River to the ends of the earth" (Zech. 9:10).

The purposes of history will thus draw to completion with the return of Christ. These, of course, may not have been the purposes of every individual, or the purposes of some powerful nation, or even some centuries' old culture. But the purposes of God will draw to completion.

It is true that students of Scripture sometimes differ in their precise understanding of this completion. Some may believe that the return of Christ will immediately signal the creation of a new heavens and a new earth. Others, like myself, believe that the triumph of Christ will first bring in a thousand-year form of the kingdom before the creation of the new heavens and new earth. But obviously both kinds of students can eagerly anticipate the Lord's triumphant return and its ultimate consummation in a new creation.

And so it is safe to say that the purposes of God do draw to completion with the victory at Megiddo, however the details of that completion are understood. For the return of Christ is the decisive, dramatic event bringing God's rule of righteousness upon the earth. And that has been His purpose since time began.[3]

A Golden Age on Earth

Then, as the prophet Daniel said, "The God of heaven will set up a kingdom which will never be destroyed, and that kingdom will not be left for another people; it will crush and put an end to all these kingdoms, but it will itself endure forever" (Dan. 2:44).

Christ will be "given dominion, glory and a kingdom, that all the peoples, nations, and men of every language might serve Him. His dominion is an everlasting dominion which will not pass away; and His kingdom is one which will not be destroyed" (Dan. 7:14).

Then, "They will hammer their swords into plowshares, and their spears into pruning hooks. Nation will not lift up sword against nation, and never again will they learn war" (Isa. 2:4). In describing this peace, Isaiah wrote that "The wolf will dwell with the lamb, and the leopard will lie down with the kid, and the calf and the young lion and the fatling together; and a little boy will lead them. Also the cow and the bear will graze; their young will lie down together; and the lion will eat straw like the ox. And the nursing child will play by the hole of the cobra, and the weaned child will put his hand on the viper's den. They will not hurt or destroy in all My holy mountain, for the earth will be full of the knowledge of the LORD as the waters cover the sea" (Isa. 11:6-9).

In a very picturesque way, Isaiah has told us that those who normally are in conflict will be at peace in the kingdom. And, consequently, the kingdom will be characterized by happiness and rejoicing. In fact, Isaiah pictured this happiness in a description of a joyous feast inaugurating the kingdom. "The Lord of hosts will prepare a lavish banquet for all peoples on this mountain; a banquet of aged wine, choice pieces with marrow, and refined, aged wine. And on this mountain He will swallow up the covering which is over all peoples, even the veil which is stretched over all nations. He will swallow up death for all time, and the LORD GOD will wipe tears away from all faces, and He will remove the reproach of His people from all the earth; for the LORD has spoken. And it will be said in that day, 'Behold, this is our God for whom we have waited that He might save us. This is the LORD for whom we have waited; let us rejoice and be glad in His salvation' " (Isa. 25:6-9).

VIOLENCE AND PEACE

Of course, the peace, joy, and prosperity will not come without the war, sorrow, and destruction preceding it in the Battle of Armageddon. And for many people, this fact has raised a serious question: How can a God of love use such violent means to achieve His purpose?

Those questioners must first realize that although God's means may be violent, they are not unfair. Quite the contrary; they represent the highest exercise of His justice. For it is only just to eventually punish the guilt of those who continually reject His mercy. And certainly the guilt of rebellion rests upon the demonically inspired armies who fight against their Creator at Armageddon.

How can a God of love fight the Battle of Armageddon? Because He is first of all a God of goodness. And if He is good, then He is not only loving but also just. And a just God must punish the ones who refuse His mercy.

Perhaps this answer is not an easy one to grasp. And that may be one reason the writers of the New Testament were careful to show us not only the love of Christ but also His justice. For if we could see the sense of justice in His character at His first coming, then perhaps we would not be so surprised at its display at His second coming.

John in his gospel, for example, showed the reader this quite plainly. He began by saying that Jesus was "full of grace and truth" (1:14). He meant that Jesus had not only the warmth of love and grace but also the firmness of justice and truth in His character. Then first he highlighted the grace of Christ in the miraculous transformation of water to wine at the wedding feast in Cana (2:1-11). But then he immediately followed that with a graphic display of truth when he recounted the just anger of Christ in clearing out the profaned Temple precincts with a whip of cords (2:13-22).

SYMMETRY

With artistic balance, John proceeded to show this same grace and truth woven together in the tapestry of two private conversations that follow the two public events just described. In the first, Christ spoke with a man named Nicodemus (3:1-21). And in the second, He conversed with the unnamed woman at the well in Samaria (4:1-30).

It appears that John intended us to contrast the two interviews.[4] For he has set both private conversations in contrast to the two preceding public events. And yet within the two talks, he has drawn artistic contrasts. Nicodemus was (1) a man, (2) at the top of the social ladder, (3) a leader in Israel, (4) who sought Christ, (5) by night. On the other hand, the encounter at Sychar was with (1) a woman, (2) at the bottom of the social ladder, (3) an unnamed outcast of Samaria, (4) sought by Christ, (5) at midday.

But not only are the scenes in stark contrast. More significantly, John has skillfully portrayed a gentle contrast in the grace and truth of Christ in these conversations. To both, Christ offered the gift of life. But to Nicodemus the firmness and strength of truth were shown initially. And to the woman the generosity and love of grace were shown initially. For Christ told proud Nicodemus, the ruler in Israel, that his accomplishments others thought were great, in reality did nothing to gain him eternal life. He must be born again, start over completely.

But to the defeated, lonely woman at the well the same message of eternal life was expressed initially in terms of grace. Eternal life, Jesus assured her, is a gift taken as simply as a drink of water is taken to quench one's thirst.

However, it is not only in the beginning of the conversations that we see the contrast. For soon Christ would, in grace, offer to Nicodemus the gift of life through faith (3:16). And equally as soon He would, in truth, confront the woman of Samaria with her sin to awaken her to her need for forgiveness and new life (4:16-19). But Jesus knew exactly the right moment to do both. He knew precisely when grace or truth should be accented in the conversations, just as He knew with which one to begin.

At the wedding feast in Cana and the cleansing of the Temple, we see quite clearly the difference between grace and truth. But in these two private conversations, we are aware of the perfect symmetry with which they are woven together in the character of Christ.

It thus becomes more clear why Christ could display His justice as easily as His love. Both were inseparably united in His character. And, consequently, He could also proclaim a message of judgment as clearly as one of grace.

For example, when Jesus was confronted by the unrelenting hypocrisy and pride of the religious leaders of His day, He sounded judgment upon them more severe than the severest of prophets. "Blind guides . . . hypocrites . . . fools . . . brood of vipers," He accused them. "How shall you escape the sentence of hell? . . . You are like whitewashed tombs which on the outside appear beautiful, but inside they are full of dead men's bones and all uncleanness" (Matt. 23:1-36, esp. 27, 33).

So the same Son of God who in grace made water into wine also in justice could clear out the Temple. The same Son of God who spoke in grace and truth to Nicodemus and the Samaritan woman will speak in grace and truth at His return. For in truth, He who was not reluctant to proclaim judgment shall not hesitate to perform it at Armageddon. And then in grace He shall bring His own into the kingdom He has gained.

THE GOLDEN LION

In the fairy tales of Narnia by C. S. Lewis, Aslan the golden lion represents the person of Christ. And in the description of this fierce lion, Lewis has captured the twin sides of Christ's character in a remarkable way. One such picture is given when the children in the imaginary land of Narnia had just heard from the beavers about the wonderful and fearful Aslan. Then they are promised they shall meet him.

"Is he—quite safe?" Susan said, "I shall feel rather nervous about meeting a lion."

"That you will, dearie, and no mistake," said Mrs. Beaver, "if there's anyone who can appear before Aslan without their knees knocking, they're either braver than most or else just silly."

"Then he isn't safe?" said Lucy.

"Safe?" said Mr. Beaver. "Don't you hear what Mrs. Beaver tells you? Who said anything about safe? 'Course he isn't safe. But he's good. He's the king, I tell you."[5]

After the children finally met Aslan, Lucy observed that his paws were potentially very soft or very terrible. They could be as soft as velvet with his claws drawn in, or sharp as knives with his claws extended.[6]

The biblical portrait of Christ is much the same. He is

not safe and harmless, but He *is* good. And His touch can be as soft as velvet or as piercing as the claw of a lion. For, as John has written, Christ is full of grace *and* truth.

And our grasp of this should dispel any misgivings about the significance of the battle beside the Mount of Megiddo. For that battle will not only be a decisive step in the fulfillment of God's purposes; it will also be a dramatic display of the true character of Christ. So with misgivings removed and the character of Christ in focus, perhaps we now may take an unobstructed view of His return. With unrestrained appreciation, we may look upon the colorful portrait of the Warrior from heaven, the fifth and final image of the miraculous mirror.

THE HERO OF REVELATION

Although several such pictures are given to us by the authors of Scripture, perhaps none is so spectacular as that one presented in Revelation. In the climactic chapter of that book is a description of the conquering Lord that may be the most breath-taking picture of all (Rev. 19:11-16).

And I saw heaven opened; and behold, a white horse, and He who sat upon it is called Faithful and True; and in righteousness He judges and wages war. And His eyes are a flame of fire, and upon His head are many diadems; and He has a name written upon Him which no one knows except Himself. And He is clothed with a robe dipped in blood; and His name is called The Word of God. And the armies which are in heaven, clothed in fine linen, white and clean, were following Him on white horses. And from His mouth comes a sharp sword, so that with it He may smite the nations; and He will rule them with a rod of iron; and He treads the wine press of the fierce wrath of God, the Almighty. And on His robe and on His thigh He has a name written, "KING OF KINGS, AND LORD OF LORDS."

Of course, no picture is fully appreciated until it is placed against is proper background. And this picture from Revelation is no exception. For this scene from heaven must be set against the corresponding scene on earth, if we are to really grasp its meaning.

THE PLANET OF DEATH

And what a startling background the earth provides. It is filled with hatred, fear, and death. Earthquakes have crumbled its buildings. Disease has ravaged its people. War has destroyed land and populace. Famine has brought weakness or death to all but the wealthy elite. The terror of anarchy has filled the streets. And many choose suicide over the agony of life (Rev. 6). As it was foretold by the prophet Isaiah, "The earth is broken asunder, the earth is split through, the earth is shaken violently. The earth reels to and fro like a drunkard, and it totters like a shack, for its transgression is heavy upon it, and it will fall, never to rise again" (Isa. 24:19-20).

But these earth-devastating disasters are only the natural ones. Supernatural catastrophes also have terrorized the planet. Destructive forces from the heavens have destroyed a third of the land. A power greater than a nuclear blast has destroyed a third of the oceans when "something like a great mountain burning with fire was thrown into the sea" (Rev. 8:8). A similar weapon has destroyed the fresh water supplying the rivers and streams. And cosmic cataclysms apparently have altered the orbital patterns of the planets (Rev. 8:11-13).

The supernatural calamities, however, have gone beyond the purely physical realm. The earth has also been filled with the horror of demonic forces unleashed by Satan for hideous torture of mankind. "Their torment was like the torment of a scorpion when it stings a man." And so horrible was their torture that "In those days men will seek death and will not find it; and they will long to die and death flees from them" (Rev. 9:5-6).

Demonic forces have also empowered a massive army of 200 million soldiers who destroy vast areas of the Eastern Hemisphere. In their bloody path, a third of mankind lay brutally destroyed. World War II caused the deaths of 55 million people. But this one army will have brought the deaths of twenty times that many (Rev. 9:13-19).

As impossible as it seems, however, the worst horrors have not yet been described. There is at the end a cancerous plague that affects nearly a billion people, a pollution of the oceans so severe that no creature in it can live, an increase in solar heat so intense that men are scorched by its intensity, and, finally, a military conflict so comprehensive that all the armies of the earth will march to destroy one another (Rev. 16:1-16).

That is the background on earth which Revelation's portrait of Christ from heaven must be set against. For it is shortly after the armies have gathered against one another that they turn to fight against the Lord who then appears in the sky. But just before His appearance a strange event foreshadows His coming.

When Light Is Gone

A supernatural darkness envelops the entire planet. Over the smoke, rubble, and destruction settles a blanket of blackness. It is like the blanket of death one places over a corpse. Not because everyone on earth has died. But because almost all the living bear the ugliness of death. And that death and ugliness is a result of their sin.

One might have speculated that the catastrophes would have awakened all to their need for God's help. For some it did. But for most it only embittered and enraged them all the more. And their murders of men, perversions of

144

sex, and worship of Satan are but a few of the ways they expressed their hatred of God. Amidst the ugliness of destruction was their still uglier sinfulness. So over this corpse of ugliness the blanket of darkness fell.

The Lord Jesus had foretold it long ago. He had been sitting alone upon a hill above Jerusalem. And He had been thoughtfully looking over her. But then His disciples spotted Him and seized the opportunity for one of those private conversations that had become so rare in the days before the cross. They had already heard Him make some startling predictions about the destruction preceding His return. But they wanted to know more. So with curiosity burning within them, they half ran up the hill to ask Him their questions about the future (Matt. 24:1-44).

After they had blurted out more questions than He could answer all at once, He began to speak. And as He spoke in a low, firm voice about the end of the age, their intellectual curiosity was transformed into a breath-taking awe over the horrors and hopes of the future It is no wonder, for He briefly described the catastrophic scene on earth prior to His coming.

Near the end of His description, He spoke of an eerie darkness that would come over the land before He returned. "Immediately after the tribulation of those days THE SUN WILL BE DARKENED, AND THE MOON WILL NOT GIVE ITS LIGHT, AND THE STARS WILL FALL from the sky, and the powers of the heavens will be shaken" (Matt. 24:29).

It is a perfect setting for His return. For with this darkness covering the world, He will flash forth in the sky for all to see. "Just as the lightning comes from the east, and flashes even to the west," Jesus told the spellbound disciples, "so shall the coming of the Son of Man be" (24:27). So there need be no doubt whatsoever about the authenticity of someone claiming to be Christ in the present day; it is impossible that any self-styled messiah could be who he claims. For Christ's return will be a public event known to all.

In fact, Christ forewarned His followers against those who claim He would come the second time in obscurity. "If anyone says to you, 'Behold, here is the Christ,' or 'There He is,' do not believe him. For false Christs and false prophets will arise and will show great signs and wonders, so as to mislead, if possible, even the elect. Behold, I have told you in advance. If therefore they say to you, 'Behold, He is in the wilderness,' do not go forth, or, 'Behold, He is in the inner rooms,' do not believe them" (Matt. 24:23-26). Christ will not return to be in the wilderness, as was John the Baptist. Nor will He return to be in the inner rooms of a manger, as He was in Bethlehem. But with darkness settled upon the earth, He will appear in the sky, and the only light in all creation will brilliantly shine upon Him.

STARS AND SUPERSTARS

As a theater darkens before the spotlight shines on the star performer, so earth's stage will be darkened before the most magnificent spotlight in the universe shines upon its only true Superstar. All the world will see this final image in the miraculous mirror. And that is what John saw when he began his description of the conquering Lord, in Revelation 19:11-16. "I saw heaven opened," he began. And what a sight it must have been.

Others had, on rare occasions, seen something remotely similar. When the heavens parted for the prophet Ezekiel, he saw visions of God (Ezek. 1:24-28). When the heavens opened at the baptism of Christ, the Spirit descended in the form of a dove, and the Father's voice identified the Son (Matt. 3:16-17). Finally, when the heavens opened for Stephen as he was martyred, he saw Christ standing at the right hand of the Father (Acts 7:55-56). But only on those rare occasions, did that fifth dimension where God dwelt visibly break into the four dimensions of creation. And never so dramatically as this.

"O that [You would tear] the heavens and come down," Isaiah had prayed, "that the mountains might quake at [Your] presence—as fire kindles the brushwood, as fire causes water to boil—to make [Your] name known to [Your] adversaries, that the nations may tremble at [Your] presence" (Isa. 64:1-2).

THE NAMES OF GOD

John saw the spectacular preview of the answer to that prayer. Yet not only did he see it in the tearing of the heavens, but also in God's making known His name to His adversaries. And this means that God made known His character to the people of the earth. For in the ancient world, a person's name expressed his character. "Abraham," for example, means "father of a multitude," and that was the name of the father of the nation Israel. "David" means "beloved," and that was the name of a king specially loved by God. "Solomon" came from the word for "peace," and that was the name of a king whose reign was full of peace. So if God makes known His name, then He, in effect, reveals His character. And that is exactly what will happen at Christ's return. His name and character will be revealed.

In fact, four different names were given to Christ in the portrait described by John. And each one captured a different aspect of His character.

A NAME TO COUNT ON

The first was given when John saw the heavens opened. For John wrote, "And behold, a white horse, and He who sat upon it is called Faithful and True; and in righteousness He judges and wages war" (Rev. 19:11).

147

The aspect of Christ's character revealed by this name is easy to see. He is called Faithful and True, because He is faithful to His Father and to His people and, therefore, true to every promise He makes. And the particular promise He fulfills when given this name is His promise to return as a conquering King to save His people and defeat His enemies.

Was Christ faithful to fulfill the promises of His first coming? There is no doubt that He was. And one may be just as confident that Christ will be equally faithful to fulfill the promises of His return. Consequently, He will be faithful to His promise of victory. And the portrayal of Him upon a white horse assures us of it. For in the ancient world, the white horse was a victor's symbol. The victorious Persian Xerxes, for example, rode on white Nisaean horses (Herodotus 7:40). And four white horses drew the chariot of Caesar in his triumphant march through Rome. Also in the book of Revelation the temporary success of a major military leader is symbolized by the white horse of victory (Rev. 6:2). However, no one shall ride it more deservedly than Christ at His return.

Yet Christ deserves the name Faithful and True for another reason, too. For He is faithful not only to His promise of victory but also to His character of justice. And this John quickly added, "And in righteousness He judges and wages war." Notice that judicial decision precedes military action. First He judges; then He wages war. And He does both in righteousness. In righteousness, He judges every aspect of the offense; and in righteousness, He executes the penalty in war. So when He battles, He is not irrational from vengeance but justly angry with sin. In justifiable anger, He cleanses the earth from those who oppose their Creator. And in so doing, He is Faithful and True to His character of justice.

Of course, there are some aspects of His character no one will ever comprehend in full. As a child may not comprehend in full the character of his father, or a student the wisdom of his teacher, so no man can comprehend in full the character of Christ. We are all like children before Him. And, therefore, to us the depth of His character must always remain a mystery.

A Name of Mystery

That is why the second name of Christ in John's description is a name of mystery. For after calling Christ Faithful and True, he said of Christ that "His eyes are a flame of fire, and upon His head are many diadems; and He has a name written upon Him which no one knows except Himself" (Rev. 19:12). Remember that a name grasped an element of a person's character. So if this name cannot be comprehended, then it means there is an element of Christ's character that cannot be comprehended. Only God the Father, Son, and Holy Spirit can fully understand the depths of their character and the full meaning of their actions.

Nevertheless, we still may learn much from this incomprehensible name. For this name implies, first of all, that Christ is supreme in understanding. He knows that which no one else knows. He understands every man, but no man fully understands Him. The Scriptures describe a man whose perspective is from God as a man who "appraises all things, yet he himself is appraised by no man" (1 Cor. 2:15). In the ultimate sense, Christ is this Man, because He is the God-Man. Only He is supreme in understanding.

But the incomprehensible name also means that He is supreme in power. For in the ancient world, it was often thought that knowledge of a god's name gave one power over him. So if no one knows this name of Christ, then it means that no one has power over Him.

Perhaps it should not surprise us, however, that the one

supreme in knowledge and wisdom is also supreme in power. For the more knowledgeable man frequently has greater power in the exercise of strategy whether on the chessboard, the football field, or the battlefield. And the wise man also will frequently have the power of depth and strength of character. So it is quite reasonable that Christ, who is supreme in knowledge and wisdom, is also supreme in power. For He has the most brilliant mind and the strongest character in the universe.

That is the meaning of the name which no one knows except Himself. Christ is supreme in wisdom and power. And that, incidentally, is why John, in the same breath as the mention of that name, said of Christ that "His eyes are a flame of fire, and upon His head are many diadems." For with supreme knowledge and wisdom, Christ peers into the heart of a man with the burning eyes of judgment. And with supreme power, He wins the crown of every king and wears their many crowns as a picture of His victory.

A NAME OF POWER

But this victory does not come without the bloodshed of battle. And that is why the next name of Christ that John disclosed is a name of bloodshed. For the third name in John's description is the title The Word of God. For us this name may appear as weak as ink on a page, but to John and his original readers it was as strong as the power that could create or destroy a universe.

For it was The Word of God that brought all the world to life when He spoke the word of creation. Yet it was also The Word of God which could bring the world to death when He spoke the word of destruction. When God brought death upon the Egyptians, for example, one popular writer of John's century described the event as the work of the sharp sword of The Word of God.

For while peaceful silence enwrapped all things,
And night in her swiftness was in mid-course,
Thine all powerful Word leaped from heaven down
from the royal throne,
A stern Warrior, into the midst of the doomed land,
Bearing as a sharp sword Thine unfeigned command-
ment
And standing, filled all things with death;
And while it touched the heaven, it trode upon the
earth.[7]

                    Wisdom of Solomon 18:15-18

For another example, when God once brought death to disobedient Israelites in the Old Testament, the book of Hebrews described it as the work of The Word of God (Heb. 4:11-12). So the title describes not only One with the power of life but also One with the power of death. And in John's description, there seems to be no question but that the emphasis is on the latter.

For when John cited this title, he described the Lord as follows: "He is clothed with a robe dipped in blood; and His name is called The Word of God. And the armies which are in heaven, clothed in fine linen, white and clean, were following Him on white horses. And from His mouth comes a sharp sword, so that with it He may smite the nations; and He will rule them with a rod of iron; and He treads the wine press of the fierce wrath of God, the Almighty" (Rev. 19:13-15).

With this description, John riveted attention upon the destructive power expressed in the title The Word of God. He had already pictured Christ as One who judges and wages war (19:11). Now he described Him as One whose robe is dipped in blood (19:13). And presumably this is the blood of His enemies. For so it is in the one Old Testament passage which describes the Messiah's robe dipped in blood—Isaiah 63:1-6—from which this passage is drawn. Furthermore, John described a spectacular army following The Word of God. And armies come for judgment, not grace.

Notice also that from His mouth comes a sharp sword. This is a figure of speech, of course, and simply means that the words of His mouth, like a sharp sword, bring the death of war. For with this word, He smites, not blesses, the nations. And He rules them with a rod of iron that punishes, not a rod of velvet that comforts. For He crushes them in His anger as one crushes grapes in a wine press. And that is why there is blood upon His robe. For elsewhere John told us that when the wine press of the battlefield was trodden "blood came out from the wine press, up to the horses' bridles, for a distance of 200 miles" (Rev. 14:20).

An ancient rabbi had written that when the Messiah came in judgment, "Kings and princes shall be slain. He will make red the rivers with the blood of the slain . . . His garments will be dipped in blood."[8] John, in Revelation, had said the same. So it is true that The Word of God is One with the power of life and death. But John saw The Word of God at His return chiefly as One with the power of death.

Yet when Christ comes in judgment, He shall not come alone. The One called The Word of God shall come with a splendrous following. "The armies which are in heaven, clothed in fine linen, white and clean, were following Him on white horses" (Rev. 19:14).

The great nations of the earth frequently display their military power with impressive military parades. Tanks and missiles slowly lumber through the streets, followed by thousands of strong, young troops. It is, one must admit, an awesome sight. Nevertheless, no nation of the earth has ever fielded an army like the one that will follow The Word of God into battle. In splendor, power, numbers, and strength that army is incomparable.

152

But who shall be in it? Some readers have thought the soldiers were men; others have believed they were angels. But the soldiers likely are both, for there is good evidence to support the inclusion of each.

ANGELIC WARRIORS

The warrior angels who were ready to come to Christ's defense in the Garden of Gethsemane (Matt. 26:53), who will battle Satan's angels in heaven (Rev. 12:7-9), and execute judgments upon the earth before Christ's return (Rev. 8; 9; 14:18-20; 16) will likely accompany Him in battle.

In fact, Christ explicitly told us they shall at least return with Him. "When the Son of Man comes in His glory, *and all the angels with Him*, then He will sit on His glorious throne" (Matt. 25:31, itals. added). It is of course possible that these angels are not in the army of heaven, and their purpose is not a military one. But elsewhere Christ implied that it is. For He clearly stated that at His return, they will obey their Commander's final battle orders: "The Son of Man will send forth His angels, and they will gather out of His kingdom all STUMBLING BLOCKS, AND THOSE WHO COMMIT LAWLESSNESS" (Matt. 13:41).

Thus not only does the power and military ability of the angels make them likely members of the cosmic army, but Christ Himself assured us they will return with Him and obediently fulfill His final orders. So it is probable that at least the mighty warrior angels will serve in the splendrous army of the One called The Word of God.

HEAVEN'S SOLDIERS FROM EARTH

But there is also good reason to believe that chosen persons of God will share that mission, too. It is implied early in the book of Revelation when Christ promised a faithful believer a special role in the kingdom. "He who overcomes, and he who keeps My deeds until the end, TO HIM I WILL GIVE AUTHORITY OVER THE NATIONS; AND HE SHALL RULE THEM WITH A ROD OF IRON, AS THE VESSELS OF THE POTTER ARE BROKEN TO PIECES, as I also have received authority from My Father" (Rev. 2:26-27).

The occasion for the breaking of the nations like a potter's vessel is the return of Christ in battle. For it is said of Christ, as Christ said of a faithful believer, that at His return to the nations of the earth, "He will rule them with a rod of iron" (Rev. 19:15). So if a faithful believer is promised a share in the authority to rule the nations with a rod of iron, and this occurs at Christ's return, then it seems reasonable that faithful believers must accompany Him into battle.

Their presence with Christ is implied in another way, too. Shortly before the description of the army comes a description of Christians as the Bride of Christ. "It was given to her to clothe herself in fine linen, bright and clean" (Rev. 19:8). Yet only six verses later, it is said of the armies from heaven that they too are "clothed in fine linen, white and clean." Of course it is possible that both men and angels could share that description. But in light of the recent description of Christians, it seems likely that John intended us to realize that faithful men are in the army from heaven, too.

But John did more than simply imply this. He seemed to explicitly tell us. For in describing the war of the nations against Christ, he wrote, "These will wage war against the Lamb, and the Lamb will overcome them, because He is Lord of lords and King of kings, and those who are with Him are the called and chosen and faithful" (Rev. 17:14). Once in Scripture, angels are designated as chosen (1 Tim. 5:21). But never are they described as "faithful" or "called." And it is easy to imagine why. An angel is never "called" out of a sinful state to a righteous one, for angels were never redeemed. Only men may be "called and chosen and faithful." So John, in Revelation, seemed not only to have implied but also to have declared that faithful men will be in the cosmic army with the warrior angels.

The title The Word of God is thus not only a title of power and justice but also one of splendor and awe. For the Commander bearing this title is a military leader followed by the only army in the universe comprised of thousands of warrior angels and faithful men.

A Story in a Word

John also used this title ingeniously to tell us one thing more. Several times we have noticed that John could be a very subtle, creative artist. And he exhibited his skill again in the use of this title to imply the completion of Christ's work. For by a very clever variation of this title in his gospel, his letters, and his revelation, he captured the story of Christ's work.

Revelation

In John's gospel, Christ was simply called the Word. "In the beginning was the Word, and the Word was with God, and the Word was God. . . . And the Word became flesh, and dwelt among us" (John 1:1, 14). By this simple title, John told a profound truth. As a word is the expression of a thought, so Christ, as God the Son, was the eternal expression of the Father. And thus as words reveal the speaker, so Christ revealed the Father.

How effectively this truth captured the heart of John's gospel. For it was expressly written to set forth Christ as the eternal Son who perfectly revealed the Father and warranted the faith of every believer (John 20:31). So how appropriate that in the gospel, the title of Christ as the Word should focus attention on Him as the One who revealed the Father. For in the gospel, Christ was the living

Word the Father had spoken. And that is why He was called the Word in John's gospel.

LIFE

But in John's first letter, he wrote not to convert men to belief but to encourage those who had believed. The ones to whom he wrote had learned already that Christ is the eternal Word who is the Revealer of the Father. Furthermore, they had believed in Him and discovered personally that He was also the Giver of eternal life. And it is the rich potential of that life in Christ that is the subject of the letter. Consequently, to reflect the heart of his first letter, John did not call Christ simply the Word, but rather the Word *of Life*, for by that title He should be known by every believer (1 John 1:1). Thus by a slight but artistic variation on the previous title, he had captured the heart of his letter and the purpose of Christ's first coming—to bring life to those who would take it.

JUDGMENT

Of course, when one comes to the book of Revelation, he has passed from the emphasis on life received by believers to an emphasis on judgment given to unbelievers. And, therefore, it is not surprising that by another artistic variation on the title, John captured the emphasis of his subject again. For in Revelation, Christ was given the title we have seen associated with the power of death and destruction. He was called the mighty Word of God. And that title thus captured the completion of Christ's work in judgment.

He came first as the Word who revealed the Father. Those who believed in Him then knew Him as the Word of Life. Those who reject Him will know Him as the awesome Word of God. For the eternal Word, one must always remember, is not only a God of grace and life, but also a God of truth and justice.

The title of Christ as The Word of God should always remind us of that. For it is not simply a title of power and judgment, nor merely one given as He comes with the splendrous army from heaven. But it is also a title which reminds us that the One who brings judgment has also brought the revelation of the Father and eternal life to anyone willing to receive it.

As rich in meaning as that title is, however, it must bow with all else to the impressiveness of the final title given to Christ in the portrait of His return. And John incorporates that title into the climactic conclusion of his description.

A NAME OF MAJESTY

"And from His mouth comes a sharp sword, so that with it He may smite the nations; and He will rule them with a rod of iron; and He treads the wine press of the fierce wrath of God, the Almighty. And on His robe and on His thigh He has a name written, 'KING OF KINGS, AND LORD OF LORDS' " (Rev. 19:15-16).

King of kings and Lord of lords—the authority and power that make this title a reality is described in the first of John's final sentences. John's artistic ingenuity is never more evident, for the description in that one sentence is a tapestry woven from four beautiful fabrics of Old Testament prophecy. A phrase from each of four prophecies became threads he wove together into one harmonious description of the power of Christ.

The Old Testament passages John drew upon were very carefully chosen, too. Each one is a famous passage on the coming of the kingdom. It comes climactically, of course, only with the coming of the king in power. So each of these kingdom passages offers a description of that power which John described in his portrait of Christ.

By this artistry, therefore, John did more than describe Christ's power. He also focused every reader's attention upon the Old Testament passages describing the effect of that power which is to bring in a magnificent kingdom over all the earth. Since Christ will reign over that kingdom, and the passages describing the power of Christ focus attention upon the kingdom, they truly show He deserves the title King of kings and Lord of lords. And that is what John intended we see.

But John's first readers saw this more quickly than we, however, since they were more familiar with the Old Testament. When they read the description of the power of Christ, their minds naturally turned to the Old Testament context of the phrases in that description. Their minds turned to them as naturally as a phrase from a popular song turns our attention upon the melody and words of an entire song.

In order for us to have the same experience as they in reading John's description, then, we must first be aware of the four great passages from which John wove his tapestry, in verse 15. And, therefore, the origin of each thread of the tapestry is given in parenthesis.

"And from His mouth comes a sharp sword (Isa. 49:1-13), so that with it He may smite the nations (Isa. 11:1-10); and He will rule them with a rod of iron (Psalm 2:1-12); and He treads the wine press of the fierce wrath of God, the Almighty" (Isa. 63:1-6).

A SWORD OF DEATH

The context for the first of John's phrases is Isaiah 49:1-13.

> Listen to Me, O islands,
> And pay attention, you peoples from afar.
> The LORD called Me from the womb;
> From the body of My mother He named Me.

158

²*And He has made My mouth like a sharp sword;*
In the shadow of His hand He has concealed Me,
And He has also made Me a select arrow;
He has hidden Me in His quiver.
³And He said to Me, "You are My Servant, Israel,
In Whom I will show My glory."
⁴But I said, "I have toiled in vain,
I have spent My strength for nothing and vanity;
Yet surely the justice due to Me is with the LORD,
And My reward with My God."

⁵And now says the LORD, who formed Me from the womb
    to be His Servant,
To bring Jacob back to Him, in order that Israel might be
    gathered to Him
(For I am honored in the sight of the LORD,
And My God is My strength),
⁶He says, "It is too small a thing that You should be
    My Servant
To raise up the tribes of Jacob, and to restore the preserved
    ones of Israel;
I will also make You a light of the nations
So that My salvation may reach to the end of the earth."
⁷Thus says the LORD, the Redeemer of Israel,
    and its Holy One,
To the despised One,
To the One abhorred by the nation,
To the Servant of rulers,
"Kings shall see and arise,
Princes shall also bow down;
Because of the LORD who is faithful, the Holy One of Israel
    who has chosen You."
⁸Thus says the LORD, "In a favorable time I have
    answered You,
And in a day of salvation I have helped You;
And I will keep You and give You for a covenant
    of the people,
To restore the land, to make them inherit the
    desolate heritages;

⁹Saying to those who are bound, 'Go forth,'
To those who are in darkness, 'Show yourselves.'
Along the roads they will feed,
And their pasture will be on all bare heights.
¹⁰"They will not hunger or thirst,
Neither will the scorching heat or sun strike them down;
For He who has compassion on them will lead them,
And will guide them to springs of water.
¹¹"And I will make all My mountains a road,
And My highways will be raised up.
¹²"Behold, these shall come from afar;
And lo, these will come from the north and from the west,
And these from the land of Sinim."
¹³Shout for joy, O heavens! And rejoice, O earth!
Break forth into joyful shouting, O mountains!
For the LORD has comforted His people,
And will have compassion on His afflicted (itals. added).

In this passage, Christ called the world to attention to tell of God's mission for Him. The means given for its accomplishment was the power of the sword of His mouth (Isa. 49:2). And this was to be exercised not only at His first coming but also at His second.

In the midst of this mission, however, Christ experienced apparent failure but affirmed His faith in the Father (49:4). Of course, the apparent failure was the cross. But then the Father assured Him that the purpose of the cross was to bring greater glory to God in Christ's bringing about not only the salvation of Israel but also all of the world (49:5-7). Then the kings of the earth "shall see and arise, princes shall also bow down" (49:7).

Furthermore, the kingdom will be a perfect one. Those in it "will not hunger or thirst, neither will the scorching heat or sun strike them down" (49:10). The heavens, the earth and its mountains will shout for joy (49:13). That is the kingdom of the One with a mouth like a sharp sword. And that is why He deserved the title King of kings and Lord of lords.

The second phrase in John's description, "So that with it
[the sword] He may smite the nations," justified that title,
too. And we may see why when we read the context from
which it was taken (Isa. 11:1-10).

> Then a shoot will spring from the stem of Jesse,
> And a branch from His roots will bear fruit.
> ²And the Spirit of the LORD will rest on Him,
> The spirit of wisdom and understanding,
> The spirit of counsel and strength,
> The spirit of knowledge and the fear of the LORD.
> ³And He will delight in the fear of the LORD,
> And He will not judge by what His eyes see,
> Nor make a decision by what His ears hear;
> ⁴But with righteousness He will judge the poor,
> And decide with fairness for the afflicted of the earth;
> *And He will strike the earth with the rod of His mouth,*
> And with the breath of His lips He will slay the wicked.
> ⁵Also righteousness will be the belt about His loins,
> And faithfulness the belt about His waist.
>
> ⁶And the wolf will dwell with the lamb,
> And the leopard will lie down with the kid,
> And the calf and the young lion and the fatling together;
> And a little boy will lead them.
> ⁷Also the cow and the bear will graze;
> Their young will lie down together;
> And the lion will eat straw like the ox.
> ⁸And the nursing child will play by the hole of the cobra,
> And the weaned child will put his hand on the viper's den.
> ⁹They will not hurt or destroy in all My holy mountain,
> For the earth will be full of the knowledge of the LORD
> As the waters cover the sea.
> ¹⁰Then it will come about in that day
> That the nations will resort to the root of Jesse,
> Who will stand as a signal for the peoples;
> And His resting place will be glorious (itals. added).

In this passage, a king is promised. For Jesse was the father of King David, and a "shoot . . . from the stem of Jesse" would be a descendant of King David. Since this descendant was in the royal line of David, He would have the right by birth to rule.

But the passage declared that He would also have the right by gift. For God especially gifted Him by the Spirit to rule (v. 2). Furthermore, He would be a Ruler who not only understands justice (v. 4a) but also would have the power to execute it (v. 4b). And in describing this power, Isaiah wrote that Christ will one day use it "to strike the earth with the rod of His mouth."

John has obviously adapted this phrase to his first one. He had just referred to the sword of Christ's mouth. And this meant that His word was a sharp instrument of judgment. So instead of saying Christ strikes the earth with the rod of His mouth, he just as well has said that with the *sword* of His mouth He strikes the nations. So when a student of the Old Testament read John's phrase, his mind would immediately turn to Isaiah's prophecy.

And there he would again be reminded of the great kingdom that Christ would bring. For Isaiah described it as a place of universal peace (vv. 6-8) where "the earth will be full of the knowledge of the LORD as the waters cover the sea" (v. 9). So this second phrase, like the first, would certainly justify John's title of Christ as King of kings and Lord of lords.

A ROD OF IRON

The third phrase does the same. For "He will rule them with a rod of iron" is drawn from Psalm 2,[9] one of the most famous kingdom passages in the Old Testament.

Why are the nations in an uproar,
And the peoples devising a vain thing?
²The kings of the earth take their stand,

And the rulers take counsel together
Against the LORD and against His Anointed:
³"Let us tear their fetters apart,
And cast away their cords from us!"

⁴He who sits in the heavens laughs,
The LORD scoffs at them.
⁵Then He will speak to them in His anger
And terrify them in His fury:
⁶"But as for Me, I have installed My King
Upon Zion, My holy mountain."

"I will surely tell of the decree of the LORD;
He said to Me, "Thou art My Son,
Today I have begotten Thee.
⁸'Ask of Me, and I will surely give the nations as Thine inher-
itance,
And the very ends of the earth as Thy possession.
⁹'*Thou shalt break them with a rod of iron,*
Thou shalt shatter them like earthenware."

¹⁰Now therefore, O kings, show discernment;
Take warning, O judges of the earth.
¹¹Worship the LORD with reverence,
And rejoice with trembling.
¹²Do homage to the Son, lest He become angry, and you
perish in the way,
For His wrath may soon be kindled.
How blessed are all who take refuge in Him! (Itals. added.)

This psalm begins by describing a conspiracy that has
formed against the Lord and His anointed King (vv. 1-3).
The King's security, however, is grounded in the power
and authority of the God who made Him King (vv. 4-6). It
was the Lord who made Him King, and it was the Lord
who would keep Him King.

Then the King recounts a promise given to Him by the
Lord (vv. 7-9). And part of that promise was a guarantee

of victory over the nations when He would "rule (or break) them with a rod of iron."[10] That, of course, is the phrase John quotes.

The psalm then ends with an encouragement for all to worship the Son in the grace of the present, lest they perish in the anger of the future (vv. 10-12). But this psalm, like the other passages, also focuses one's hopes on the future kingdom. For the King is promised the "nations as [His] inheritance, and the very ends of the earth as [His] possession." And so the phrase from Psalm 2, as the previous phrases, would turn one's attention to the kingdom Christ will bring, and would assure the reader once again that Christ deserves the title King of kings and Lord of lords.

THE WRATH OF GOD

The final phrase of John's tapestry was designed to convince the reader, too. For "He treads the wine press of the fierce wrath of God, the Almighty" is drawn from one of Scripture's most vivid and startling passages on the inception of the kingdom, Isaiah 63:1-6.

> Who is this who comes from Edom,
> With garments of glowing colors from Bozrah,
> This One who is majestic in His apparel,
> Marching in the greatness of His strength?
> "It is I who speak in righteousness, mighty to save."
> 2Why is Your apparel red,
> And Your garments like the one who treads
>   in the wine press?
> 3"I have trodden the wine trough alone,
> And from the peoples there was no man with Me.
> I also trod them in My anger,
> And trampled them in My wrath;
> And their lifeblood is sprinkled on My garments,
> And I stained all My raiment.
> 4"For the day of vengeance was in My heart,

And My year of redemption has come.
5"And I looked, and there was no one to help,
And I was astonished and there was no one to uphold;
So My own arm brought salvation to Me;
And My wrath upheld Me.
6"And I trod down the peoples in My anger,
And made them drunk in My wrath,
And I poured out their lifeblood on the earth."

The prophet first presented the reader with an impressive warrior, coming from the land of Edom (v. 1). When he asked the reason for the warrior's bright red garments (v. 2), the answer was enough to startle even the most immovable person. For His battle garments were red from the dye of blood He had shed in treading the wine press of the wrath of God (vv. 3-5). "I trod down the peoples in My anger," the Victor shouted, "and made them drunk in My wrath, and I poured out their lifeblood on the earth" (v. 6). So when John's first-century reader saw the fourth phrase in John's tapestry, his mind shot back to the stunning description of victory described by Isaiah.

And, of course, he knew this would bring in the kingdom Isaiah so frequently described as, for example, in Isaiah 65:17-25. So once again, John had shown Christ worthy of the title King of kings and Lord of lords.

GOD AND MAN

One last consideration shows Him worthy again. In the Old Testament, a variation on that title was a title of God. For in Deuteronomy 10:17, God is called the God of gods and the Lord of lords. But since Christ was not only man but also God, He deserves that title, too. So not only do the Old Testament contexts of John's four phrases but also the use of the title itself in the Old Testament show Christ deserving to be called King of kings and Lord of lords.

How could such a Warrior fail to be victorious? No

wonder John concluded his description of Christ with these words, "On His robe and on His thigh He has a name written, 'KING OF KINGS, AND LORD OF LORDS' " (Rev. 19:16). The flashing of the name upon His thigh enables us to glimpse more vividly the portrait John saw of Christ at His return. As one scholar observed: "John sees in the vision the Divine Warrior and His heavenly horsemen—not halting but sweeping downward from heaven and onward against the serried armies of the Beast, False Prophet, and the kings of the earth, and as they thunder along, their garments stream behind them, and so on the thigh of the Leader is disclosed the name: 'King of Kings and Lord of Lords.' "[11]

This is the One in whom Christians have placed their hope and confidence. And this is the One Christians are commanded to follow—the One called Faithful and True, the One with a name no one knows except Himself, the One called The Word of God, and the One called King of kings and Lord of lords.

CHILDREN OF THE KING

And, of course, in being called to follow Christ we have also been called to reflect the character of Christ expressed by these four names. For example, Christ was Faithful and True to His Father, to man, and to Himself. Therefore so should we be.

In being faithful and true to God, we should be faithful and true to our commitment to Christ. We should have a Christlike purity of life, singleness of purpose, and perseverance in difficulty. We should choose to serve God rather than man and prefer God's approval to man's. And we should do so because we love the One called Faithful and True.

In being faithful and true to man, we should be faithful and true to our commitments to business associates,

166

friends, and, most of all, our family—our partners, our children, our parents. We should, therefore, avoid making promises that are not in our power to keep. But the promises we do make should be as binding as the firmest legal contract.

Often our hearts are so divided that we store up countless unkept promises and commitments to friends and family. Our words can become empty and meaningless to our husband or wife, our parents or our children, because our words are not backed up by our actions.

But we have been called to be faithful and true—to love our partner, to love our children, to love our parents, to be faithful to friends, and to honor our business commitments. And we have been called to do so because we were first called to follow Christ.

In being faithful and true to ourselves, we should be faithful and true to our consciences, our ideals, and our goals to follow the One who gives all three. And we should do all this because we belong to the One called Faithful and True.

But Christ also had a name that no one knew except Himself. And this meant that He was supreme in understanding and power. Although we will never be supreme in these, for only He is, we may nevertheless be distinguished by these. No one fully understood the motives of Christ or His understanding, for both His love and His understanding came from an infinite God.

But as Christians, we may certainly share in that love and understanding by responding to the love of Christ and the wisdom of the Scripture. And then, like Christ, we will be "spiritual" persons who possess a love and understanding that cannot be comprehended by those who do not know Christ (1 Cor. 2:15). And then we will also have a wisdom and depth of character that brings us a share of the power He has, too. And thus we will share in the understanding and power of the One who has a name that no one knows except Himself.

He also had the awesome name of judgment called The Word of God. And we have seen that it was part of the balance in His character of grace and truth. But so should we develop this same balance in our character.

With friends we should not only love them in grace, but in truth be firm in our commitment to them, encourage them to follow Christ, and be willing to confront them when they sin against God.

With our partner and children we should bear the same balance, and with children especially. For they need their parents' goodness toward them, and that includes both grace and truth: the acceptance and love of grace with the discipline and firmness of truth.

With all, we should also bring both grace and truth to the message of the gospel. The God of love and God of judgment are one and the same in the Scripture. And in telling others of Him, His full character should be displayed. The ones who refuse His mercy must anticipate His judgment.

And, finally, we must follow the one called King of kings and Lord of lords. He had a king's dignity and a king's destiny. And because we are His children, we should share that dignity and live in light of that destiny. Even on the cross, this King acted like a king though He was not treated like one. So instead of desiring to be treated like a king, we should seek more to be like one, too.

And one reason we should do so is because we will share His destiny. Paul once told certain argumentative Christians that their behavior was terribly inconsistent. For they were destined to rule the world, but they could not even settle small disputes among themselves (1 Cor. 6:1-8).

Many of us like to believe that we are nothing, that our decisions and choices do not matter, and that our behavior is inconsequential to anyone but ourselves. And the reason we like to believe this is because such thoughts remove the responsibility that true privilege brings.

But God has indeed made us something, and He has made our decisions matter, and our behavior important. He has called us to follow His Son and share in His rule. He has truly given great promises and privileges to us. And it is best we accept our position and begin to conduct ourselves like sons and daughters of the King. If we Christians are to be called by the name of Christ, we should bear the character expressed by His every name.

So let us set before us the goal to be faithful and true, distinguished by wisdom, full of grace and truth, and honorable as kings and queens. And in so doing, we shall become more like the One who bears these qualities to an infinite degree.

7

PATTERNS, PRIDE, AND PROMISES

The door of life is a door of mystery. For it magically becomes slightly shorter than the one who wishes to enter it. And thus only he who bows in humility can cross its threshold.

The victory of the Allied forces in North Africa signaled a turning point in the early stages of World War II. After this crucial campaign, Winston Churchill made one of his most memorable statements: "This is not the end. This is not the beginning of the end. But it is, perhaps, the end of the beginning."

We might say the same words after surveying in the miraculous mirror the five important images of the Son of God. We have certainly not come to the end, nor to the beginning of the end. For the long road of practicing what we have learned still lies before us. But we are perhaps at the end of the beginning. For now at least we know the direction in which we want our life and character to proceed.

And we must keep that direction clearly placed before us. But how shall we keep in mind the details of Christ's character as revealed in every image? Of course, the simplest way to recall anything is to remember a picture of it. But we have at least five pictures to remember, so that method is not as much help as it might have been.

Unless, perhaps, there is a pattern common to every picture which unifies them all. Then by remembering that one pattern, we could review each image easily.

PATTERNS

For the perceptive reader, sensitive to the character of Christ, such a pattern is, I believe, clear to see. The pattern reappears in every image as the melody of a song may recur in every verse, and, like a song melody, becomes enriched and embellished with variations of depth and meaning. It is the pattern of humility before exaltation, and it is found in each event we have considered.

Think back to His baptism in the waters of judgment. In humility, He left the comfort and peace of Galilee; in humility, He was baptized by John; and in humility, He identified with the sins of His nation. But in exaltation, the Father proclaimed Him His beloved Son and Priest and King. And in exaltation, the Father sent the Spirit upon Him.

Next, look back to His temptation in the wilderness of conflict. In humility, He fasted in repentance for the sins of the nation; and in humility, He trusted in the Father through Satan's temptations, refusing the fulfillment of God's promises not granted in God's timing, and rejecting angelic assistance that would bring Him national honor. But in exaltation at the temptation's end, the Father sent the angels to help Him, and this foreshadowed His ultimate exaltation at His return.

Now recall His transformation on the mountain of splendor. In humility, He had publicly proclaimed to His disciples His future suffering and death. And in humility, He had also called His followers to choose a similar path for themselves. But in exaltation, on the mountain, the Father transformed Him with Moses and Elijah as a picture of His future glory. And in exaltation, the Father spoke from heaven and identified His Son as the true Prophet, Priest, and King.

Remember, too, the cross on the hill of sacrifice. The pattern is perhaps easiest to see here. For in humility, Christ submitted to unfair trials, degradation, and shame, and in humility, He submitted to agonizing death and punishment for others' sins. But in exaltation, the Father resurrected Him, and in exaltation, the Father enthroned Christ beside Him in heaven.

And, finally, remember the plain of battle. The pattern is perhaps most difficult to see here, but only if we do not look back far enough. For the promise of victory in that battle was given to Christ long ago, when He was first seated in heaven in the presence of the Father (Psalm 110:1). Then in humble patience, He has waited all these years to fight that battle and bring His kingdom to us. But in exaltation, He, indeed, shall fight that battle, and in exaltation, He shall be crowned King of kings and Lord of lords.

The Pattern Begins

We should not be surprised that each episode begins with an act of humility. For so His very life began. In an astonishing expression of humility, He left His existence in heaven and became a baby in a manger. His birth was nothing less than the birth of the eternal God who took upon Himself flesh and blood. St. Augustine, one of the most perceptive Christian authors of all time, eloquently wrote of this humility many centuries ago:

> The Word of the Father, by whom all time was created, was made flesh and was born in time for us. He, without whose divine permission no day completes its course, wished to have one day for His human birth. In the bosom of His Father, He existed before all the cycles of ages; born of an earthly mother, He entered upon the

course of the years on this day.

The Maker of man became man that He, Ruler of the stars, might be nourished at the breast; that He, the Bread, might be hungry; that He, the Fountain, might thirst; that He, the Light, might sleep; that He, the Way, might be wearied by the journey; that He, the Truth, might be accused by false witnesses; that He, the Judge of the living and the dead, might be brought to trial by a mortal judge; that He, Justice, might be condemned by the unjust; that He, Discipline, might be scourged with whips; that He, the Foundation, might be suspended upon a cross; that Courage might be weakened; that Security might be wounded; that Life might die.

To endure these and similar indignities for us, to free us, unworthy creatures, He who existed as the Son of God before all ages, without a beginning, deigned to become the Son of Man in these recent years. He did this although He who submitted to such great evils for our sake had done no evil and although we, who were the recipients of so much good at His hands, had done nothing to merit these benefits.[1]

Christ's humility at His birth is almost incomprehensible to us. We hesitate to step below the slightest position of which we regard ourselves deserving. Yet the eternal God, worthy of the highest worship, became a dependent child to begin a life as the God-Man that He might bring life to us. So His birth does indeed begin a life of great humility. Thus it is not surprising that each of His life's images began in humility too.

THE PATTERN'S END

Neither is it surprising that each of those images concluded in exaltation. For as the humility beginning each image was foreshadowed by His birth, so the exaltation in each image foreshadowed His ultimate glorification at His return. And, of course, as His birth was the greatest act of humility, so His return will be the greatest scene of exaltation.

For it is the most dramatic of contrasts with the humility that preceded it in His first coming. Think of it for a moment. In His first coming, He sat upon a small donkey as He humbly offered Himself as the King. But at His second coming, He is portrayed as sweeping down from heaven on a galloping white horse of victory.

In His first coming, the angels in the army of heaven were restrained from helping Christ when He was taken by the Romans and the Israelite conspirators. But at His second coming, not only the warrior-angels but faithful men will return in the splendrous army of the Messiah to join Him in battle.

In His first coming, a supernatural darkness settled over the earth when He was crucified, and it foreshadowed the darkness of sin He would bear in place of others. The judgment of God would fall upon Him. But in His second coming, a supernatural darkness will settle on this planet to foreshadow Christ's devastation of the rebels on the earth. The judgment of God will fall upon them.

In His first coming, His own blood fell upon His garments. But at His second coming, the blood of His enemies will drip from His robe. And whereas at His first coming, a crown of thorns was thrust upon His head, at His second coming, the crown of every king will rest upon Him. So one reason Christ's return is the greatest scene of exaltation is because that scene offers the most dramatic of contrasts with the humility that preceded it.

But it is also the greatest exaltation because it fulfills the purposes of Christ's life. And in a special way it particularly fulfills the hopes and expectations of the first four images in the miraculous mirror.

The baptism pictured Christ passing through the waters of judgment. God had brought stable land out of the waters of judgment, in Genesis 1. He had brought Noah safely through the waters of judgment. And through Moses, He had brought Israel through the waters of judgment. Then Christ too passed through the waters of judgment at His baptism, thus showing not only that He would do so in reality in His death and resurrection, but also that all who belonged to Him would do the same.

But, of course, every one who belongs to Christ still awaits the fulfillment of that in his own resurrection at the return of Christ. And then, not only in hope but in reality, every believer will have passed completely through the waters of judgment, and the picture of Christ's baptism will be fulfilled in his life.

After Moses led Israel through the Red Sea waters of judgment, everyone sang praises to God for the rescue He had performed. The song they sang was called the song of Moses (Exod. 15:1-18). In celebration of Christ's rescue of believers through the waters of judgment, the same song will be sung again. For in the book of Revelation, John saw a picture of believers standing victoriously over the waters of judgment and singing the song of Moses.

"And I saw, as it were, a sea of glass mixed with fire, and those who had come off victorious from the beast and from his image and from the number of his name, standing on the sea of glass, holding harps of God. And they sang the song of Moses, the bond-servant of God and the song of the Lamb, saying, 'GREAT AND MARVELOUS ARE THY WORKS, O LORD GOD, THE ALMIGHTY; RIGHTEOUS AND TRUE ARE THY WAYS, THOU KING OF THE NATIONS. WHO WILL NOT FEAR, O LORD, AND GLORIFY THY NAME? FOR THOU ALONE ART HOLY; FOR ALL THE NATIONS WILL COME AND WORSHIP BEFORE THEE, FOR THY RIGHTEOUS ACTS HAVE

BEEN REVEALED' " (Rev. 15:2-4).

Thus John pictured the fulfillment of the hopes and expectations that were raised when Christ passed through the waters of judgment at the Jordan.

A Better Time, a Better Place

But the return of Christ will also fulfill the hopes and expectations that were inspired when Christ passed through the temptations of Satan in the wilderness of conflict. That victory took on special meaning when set against the background of David's victory over Goliath, Israel's failure in the wilderness, and Adam's sin in the Garden of Eden. Like David, Christ would defeat the enemy of His people. Unlike Israel, He would succeed and bring blessing to all the nations. Unlike Adam, He would bring not death but life to the world. At Christ's return all these expectations will be fulfilled. Satan will be decisively defeated. Blessing will come in full to the nations. And the entire new creation will overflow with life that Christ brings.

Furthermore, each prize from Satan that Christ refused will be His in a better way from the Father. Whereas Satan suggested food gained in an improper way in the temptation, at Christ's return He will celebrate in a great Messianic banquet (Isa. 25:6). Satan offered bread; God will give a feast.

Whereas Satan suggested national honor gained by the display of angelic aid were Christ to leap from the pinnacle of the Temple, at Christ's return not only will the angelic assistance be His in splendrous way, but the nation of Israel will respond to Him out of repentance and not out of superficial astonishment. Satan offered the acclaim of the mob; God promised a nation redeemed from sin.

And whereas Satan offered all the kingdoms of the earth

to Christ were He to worship him, at Christ's return all the kingdoms of the earth will be His because of His obedience to the Father. Satan offered a bribe; God will give a reward. So the anticipations of Christ's victory in the wilderness of conflict will certainly be fulfilled at His return.

HOPE AND REALITY

Of course, it is clear that the hopes of the mountain of splendor will find fulfillment at Christ's return. For that transfiguration was nothing less than a picture of that very return. Christ will descend upon a mountain with people like Moses and Elijah. Like Moses, some will have died and then return. And like Elijah, some will have never died, but will have gone to heaven immediately and then returned with Christ. And all will share that bright, brilliant radiance that Christ displayed to His disciples on the mountain of splendor.

THE KINGDOM COMES

And, finally, the purpose of the hill of sacrifice will be completed with the return of Christ. For the purpose of the cross was to regain a people and the earth for the Kingdom of God. And at the return of Christ, that Kingdom will be consummated. So it is easy to see why the return of Christ will be the greatest scene of exaltation yet. It not only will offer the most dramatic of contrasts with the humility that preceded it, but it will wonderfully fulfill the hopes and expectations of the preceding images in the miraculous mirror. And thus it is also easy to see that as the humility beginning each image was foreshadowed by the humility of His birth, so the exaltation in each image indeed foreshadowed His ultimate exaltation at His return. His life began in humility. It will conclude with exaltation. And the images in between each reflected this pattern.

A Pattern for Us

But if this pattern is fundamental to the life of Christ, then it should be fundamental to our lives, too. We originally looked for this pattern common to each image in order to more easily remember them. But what good would it do to remember each image and yet fail to practice the principle it teaches? So in order to practice this principle of humility, we must grasp what it means. And also what it does not mean.

Humility is not thinking less of yourself than you are. Nor is humility always talking about your faults and shortcomings as compared with everyone else's superiority and achievements. Humility is simply a recognition of the truth about ourselves; and then most often, a forgetfulness of self that allows genuine concern for others and a genuine worship of God.

Truth and Humility

God is the only self-sufficient, independent person that exists. He is the uncreated Creator. But everyone else, including you and me, derives life and meaning from Him. If men were the creators of truth, morals, beauty, or reality, there would be no such things as truth, morals, beauty, or reality, because every individual could make up whatever he wished to be true, good, beautiful, or real. But there is truth, reality, and goodness (else we could not even think our thoughts and imagine them right). So God must exist to sustain them, for we could not possibly be the ones who do so.

Every breath we take, every thought we think, every purpose we pursue, can only have meaning in relationship to Him. That is the truth. It is not a wishful dream nor an empty speculation. And if we, who are so dependent, would only recognize our dependence, then humility before God would be as natural as a child's respect and need for his parents.

And, of course, not only is our every breath, thought, and purpose dependent upon God, but every hope and gift we have is dependent upon the work of Christ on the cross. He forgives us, grants new life, and promises us a place in His future kingdom. So in every way, we are dependent upon God. Humility is simply a recognition of this fundamental truth.

And it is thus the most fundamental aspect of man's relationship to God. In humility, one bows to receive the forgiveness and life that begins his relationship with God. And in humility, one walks before the Creator who sustains and cares for him. But if humility is the central attitude necessary to relationship with God, then pride must be the central attitude that will prevent it. And it is easy to see why.

PRIDE AND HUMILITY

Humility seeks to bring honor to the God worthy of all honor. But pride seeks to bring honor to one's self. Humility is other-centered; pride is self-centered. Humility seeks leadership from the all-wise Creator; pride seeks self-determination. In foolish pride, a frail, unwise man prefers his own leadership to God's.

Pride is furthermore the beginning of every sin. For in pride, one exalts himself above the Creator and His will, and simply does what he desires. It was pride that caused the fall of Satan from being an angel in a place of joy and privilege to being a devil in the turmoil of hatred and condemnation (Ezek. 28:17-18; 1 Tim. 3:5-6). And it was pride that lifted the hearts of Adam and Eve above the commandment of God in Eden. So it is no wonder that the first sin in all creation was pride. It had to have been. For every other sin proceeds from it when someone exalts himself above the will of God.

PRIDE AND UNTRUTH

The results of pride are sadly predictable, too. Christ indicated that the lie would come with it (John 8:44). But that is exactly what one would expect. For if in pride a person pretends to be independent of God and above His direction, then it is inevitable that the person pretending must act out a lie. For it is a lie that he can be independent of God. He may not acknowledge it, but dependent he is.

An elephant may pretend to be an airplane. But if he said that flapping his ears were flying, he would be saying and acting a lie. And it is just as foolish for a man to pretend to be independent of God. He would be much happier and healthier if, in humility, he simply accepted his dependence and contentedly submitted to God.

PRIDE AND MURDER

But pride will not only bring the lie; it will bring also the act of murder. And Christ indicated this, too. The one who follows Satan's pride can anticipate its fruits not only in untruth but also in murder (John 8:44).

Perhaps we should have anticipated this also. For if one lives a lie then he must destroy anyone who threatens to expose it. Sometimes, of course, one may choose to murder with words instead of weapons, but one's purpose is the same—to destroy the other person and preserve one's life a bit longer.

The destruction of others through criticism rules out competition for the number one position, too. So it is not surprising that the one who lives in the untruth of pride also murders others through criticism to maintain the lie.

Humility, however, will have precisely the opposite results. Instead of pretension to be someone one is not, humility recognizes one's dependent position before God and man. Thus one lives his life in truth and not in the lie of independence.

Instead of discontent, a capacity for enjoying the present will inevitably result. A French philosopher, Pascal, noted long ago that most of us never attain that capacity. "We do not rest satisfied with the present. We anticipate that future as too slow in coming, as if in order to hasten its course; or we recall the past, to stop its too rapid flight. So imprudent are we that we dream of those times which are no more, and thoughtlessly overlook that which alone exists. For the present is generally painful to us. We conceal it from our sight, because it troubles us; and if it be delightful to us, we regret to see it pass away. We try to sustain it by the future, and think of rearranging matters which are not in our power, for a time which we have no certainty of reaching.

"Let each one examine his thoughts, and he will find them all occupied with the past and the future. We scarcely ever think of the present; and if we think of it, it is only to take light from it to arrange the future. The present is never our end. So we never live, but we hope to live; and, as we are always preparing to be happy, it is inevitable we should never be so."[2]

He has described well the discontent of most people. But the one who rests dependently in the leadership of God will have contentment, peace, and stability.

Particularly stability. As Pascal also wrote, "The great and the humble have the same misfortunes, the same griefs, the same passions; but the one is at the top of the wheel, and the other near the center, and so less disturbed by the same revolutions."[3]

182

And whereas pride brought not only untruth, but also murder, either literally or through criticism, humility will bring not only truth and peace, but also love that creates life wherever it flows. When I was a child, I read a story of a velvet rabbit owned by a young boy. The rabbit became worn, torn, and unattractive to everyone but the boy. But he loved the rabbit with all his heart. Yet one day the boy returned to his home and discovered his rabbit had been thrown away. He cried over the loss and remembered his love for his long time companion. Not long after this, a real rabbit bounded through his yard with markings so identical to his velvet rabbit's that the boy knew his velvet rabbit had become real. The point of the story, as I understand it, was that the boy's love made the velvet rabbit become real.

The story is really a modern myth because, like most ancient myths, it teaches a profound truth. People only become real when they are loved, too. And humble dependence upon God which liberates a person from self-centeredness will in turn liberate that person to love others with a love that makes them real. His love will create life.

PRIDE OR HUMILITY

Perhaps one more example will clarify the difference between pride and humility. Let us compare the two in the physical expression of love. And let us imagine that in pride a man exalts himself above the law of God and commits adultery. First of all, his expression of love is a lie because it does not flow from a life-commitment to the woman. And should the woman become pregnant, it would not be surprising if they sought abortion to hide the lie. And thus the pride of the man would have brought untruth and murder.

On the other hand, imagine that in humility a man

takes a wife, as the Scripture says, "in holiness and honor." He loves her. But beyond that, he has made a life-long commitment to her. His expression of love is thus an expression of truth. And should God bless them with a child, then their love would not only have nourished their relationship, but created life as well. "The reward of humility and the [reverence] of the Lord," the wise man wrote, "are riches, honor, and life" (Prov. 22:4). Humility will produce a love that is a fountain of life. And one certainly sees that principle in this example.

THE MAGNETISM OF CHRIST

But of course the best example is Christ Himself. For the one who is humbly dependent upon God will be freer to love, give, laugh, and sympathize than any self-centered person could ever be. That is probably one very important reason Christ had such a magnetic personality. He was so humbly dependent upon the Father that He inevitably reflected truth, peace, and love.

And that is why keeping Him before us is not only our obligation but also our delight. B. B. Warfield, one of the greatest of modern theologians, wrote that we can lovingly follow in thought every footstep of Christ. "We see Him at the banks of the Jordan, because it became Him to fulfill every righteousness, meekly receiving the baptism of repentance for us. We see Him in the wilderness, calmly rejecting the subtlest trials of the evil one: refusing to supply His needs by a misuse of His divine power, repelling the confusion of tempting God with trusting God, declining to seek His Father's ends by any other than His Father's means. We see Him among the thousands of Galilee, anointed of God with the Holy Ghost and power, going about doing good: with no pride of birth, though He was a king; with no pride of intellect, though omniscience dwelt within Him; with no pride of power, though all power in heaven and earth was in His hands; or of station, though the fulness of the Godhead dwelt in Him bodily; or of superior goodness or holiness: but in lowliness of mind esteeming everyone better than Himself, healing the sick, casting out devils, feeding the hungry, and everywhere breaking to men the bread of life. We see Him everywhere offering to men His life for the salvation of their souls: and when, at last, the forces of evil gathered thick around Him, walking, alike without display and without dismay, the path of suffering appointed for Him, and giving His life at Calvary that through His death the world might live.[4]

"He did not cultivate self, even His divine self. He took no account of self. He was not led by His divine impulse out of the world, driven back into the recesses of His own soul to brood morbidly over His own needs, until to gain His own seemed worth all sacrifice to Him. He was led by His love for others into the world, to forget Himself in the needs of others, to sacrifice self once for all upon the altar of sympathy.

"Self-sacrifice brought Christ into the world. And self-sacrifice will lead us, His followers, not away from but into the midst of men. Wherever men suffer, there will we be to comfort. Wherever men strive, there will we be to help. Wherever men fail, there will we be to uplift. Wherever men succeed, there will we be to rejoice.

"Self-sacrifice means not indifference to our times and our fellows: it means absorption in them. It means forgetfulness of self in others. It means entering into every man's hopes and fears, longings and despairs: it means manysidedness of spirit, multiform activity, multiplicity of sympathies. It means richness of development.

"It means not that we should live one life, but a thousand lives—binding ourselves to a thousand souls by the filaments of so loving a sympathy that their lives become ours. It means that all the experiences of men shall smite our souls and shall beat and batter these stubborn hearts into fitness for their heavenly home. It is, after all, then, the path to the highest possible development, by which alone we can be made truly men.

"Not that we shall undertake it with this end in view. This were to dry up its springs at their source. We cannot be self-consciously self-forgetful, selfishly unselfish. Only, when we humbly walk in this path, seeking truly in it not our own things but those of others, we shall find the promise true, that he who loses his life shall find it. Only, when, like Christ, and in loving obedience to His call and example, we take no account of ourselves, but freely give ourselves to others, we shall find, each in his measure, the saying true of himself also: 'Wherefore also God hath highly exalted Him.' The path of self-sacrifice is the path to glory."[5]

Christ's life began in humility. It will conclude in exaltation. And the images in the miraculous mirror, in between this beginning and end, each reflected this pattern. Now as we wait for His return we should reflect this pattern, too. In humble dependence we should live in grace and truth, awaiting His glorious kingdom.

Notes

Chapter 1

1. The word *katoptrizomenoi* rendered "beholding as in a mirror," has sometimes been translated "reflecting as a mirror." So instead of "But we all, with unveiled face beholding as in a mirror the glory of the Lord, are being transformed into the same image from glory to glory," the verse would read, "But we all, with unveiled face reflecting (as a mirror does) the glory of the Lord, are being transformed into the same image from glory to glory."

Although this latter rendering is admittedly possible, it seems unlikely to me for both linguistic and contextual reasons.

Linguistically, the verb in question is in the middle voice, and there are no instances in Greek literature contemporary to it where this verb in the middle voice bears the meaning "reflecting" (Kittel, T.W.N.T., II, 697).

Contextually, the passage states the result of *katoptrizomenoi* ("beholding as in a mirror" or "reflecting as a mirror") to be the transformation of the viewer into the "same image." Both "same" and "image" are significant for our decision.

The mention of "image" is clearly more consistent with a viewer beholding as in a mirror rather than his reflecting as a mirror. For if he beholds as in a mirror, then an image could be seen, but if he were reflecting as a mirror, then he himself would be the image, and, therefore no image could be seen.

The description of the image as the "same" image implies that it is an image to which he has just referred. A previous mention of an image in a mirror can be found only in the image implied in the action "beholding as in a mirror." To translate it "reflecting" would again make the viewing of an image impossible, because the viewer of the Lord would be the mirror bearing the image.

Of course, we must recall that it is an image to which he is being transformed, not an image which he already bears. So only "beholding as in a mirror" allows for an image being seen, indeed a previously mentioned image seen, an image to which one is being transformed.

For these linguistic and contextual reasons, the rendering "beholding as in a mirror" should be preferred over "reflecting as a mirror."

2. Hans Christian Anderson, "The Ugly Duckling," in *The Complete Fairy Tales and Stories,* trans. Erik Christian Hangaard (Garden City, N.Y.: Doubleday, 1974).

Chapter 2

1. Max J. Herzberg, *Myths and Their Meaning* (New York: Allyn and Bacon, 1928), p. 219.
2. This proclamation of the Father may be translated either: "This is My Son, the Beloved in whom I am well-pleased," or "This is My beloved Son, in whom I am well-pleased." One's choice is determined by the

function given *agapētos,* "beloved." This adjective may be regarded as either substantival and appositional (the first translation) or as descriptive (the second translation). The first translation has the advantage of clarifying the source of this quotation (Isa. 42:1-4 as quoted in Matt. 12:18-21). And yet it is still implied by opposition that Jesus is a "beloved Son." The descriptive force is not lost. So for clarity of source without loss of description, the first translation has been adopted.

3. Edmond Jacob, *Theology of the Old Testament,* trans. Arthur W. Heathcote and Philip J. Allcock (New York: Harper & Row, 1958), pp. 140-141.

4. The Hebrew *hōq* is frequently rendered "decree," and that is acceptable as long as one realizes it is a legal decree, or more precisely "legal statute."

5. For verification of this, one need only check the more complete quotation of Isaiah 42:1-4 in Matthew 12:18-21. Therein, one will discover that the portion of Isaiah 42:1 quoted at the baptism is a quotation from the same Greek text of Isaiah 42:1-4 used by Matthew in chapter 12. So no matter how skillful this particular Greek text was in rendering the original Hebrew (and it does seem a bit rough), it is of little consequence. Matthew clearly intends us to regard this phrase as a quotation from Isaiah 42:1.

6. Francis Brown, S. R. Driver, and Charles A. Briggs, *A Hebrew and English Lexicon of the Old Testament* (Oxford: Clarendon, 1952), p. 858.

7. The word *marat* literally means "make smooth" or "bald," perhaps by polishing as with a sword (Ezek. 21:11), or by chafing as to "rub bare the shoulder" (Ezek. 29:18). When the action is performed on the face, the manner of "making smooth" is assumed to be by plucking out, and so it is usually rendered "pluck out the beard" (Neh. 13:25). It is usually a sign

of humiliation, either self-inflicted (Ezra 9:3) or imposed by another (Neh. 13:25). This manner of "making smooth" and this humiliation may be in view here. But there is a second way to lay bare a bearded face. Repeated blows against the jaw would rub bare the cheek. And repeated blows did fall upon the cheek of the Servant on the same day He received scourging and spitting. So the verb allows for this second manner, and the fulfillment supports it; therefore, it is best translated "lay bare" not "pluck out," for this preferred translation is faithful to the meaning and yet unbiased in its suggestion of fulfillment.

8. More technically the case is as follows. The title beloved son, *agapētos huios,* occurs only six times in the Septuagint, the Greek translation of the Hebrew Old Testament. And in each instance, it translates the only six occurrences of *ben yahîd,* "only son" (Gen. 22:2, 12, 16; Jer. 6:26; Amos 8:10; Zech. 12:10). Three of these occur in Genesis 22, a fourth is clearly Messianic too (Zech. 12:10); the other two are nonspecific. So if this phrase does allude to an Old Testament context, it, in all likelihood, alludes to Genesis 22.

9. As mentioned in the text, the fact of the customary usage in Judaism of Isaac as an example of willing sacrifice makes this likelihood even more certain. This usage in Judaism may be found summarized by G. Vermes, *Scripture and Tradition in Judaism* (Leiden, 1961), pp. 193-227.

Chapter 3

1. Simonides of Ceos, *Greek Lyrics,* trans. Richard Lattimore (Chicago: University of Chicago Press, 1949), p. 55.
2. John Milton, *Paradise Regained,* Book I, II. 155-160 (from *John Milton, Complete Poems and Major Prose,* ed. Merritt Y. Hughes [New York: The Bobbs Merrill

Company, The Odyssey Press]), p. 486).

3. John Pedersen, *Israel, Its Life and Culture,* Vol. 1 (London: Oxford University Press, 1926), pp. 454-460.

4. Fasting in general expresses submission to God. In fact, the phrase "to humble the soul" means to fast (*T.W.N.T.*, 4, 927). (See Lev. 16:29, 31; 23:27, 32; Num. 29:7; Isa. 58:3.) But more particularly it is the most characteristic outward form of repentance (Jonah 3:7-8; Esther 4:16; Lev. 23:27-29; Ezra 10:6; Judg. 20:26; 1 Sam. 7:6; 2 Chron. 20:3; Joel 1:14; 2:12; Jer. 36:9; Ezra 8:21; Neh. 1:4; 2 Macc. 13:12).

5. The conclusion that this miraculous act was intended to bring recognition of Jesus as the Messiah is drawn from two lines of argument. First, the act would likely have been interpreted as a fulfillment (admittedly an untimely one from Jesus' perspective) of an indirectly Messianic psalm. And second, the structure of the temptation account itself seems to intentionally relate the second temptation to Jesus' role as the national Messiah, the Son of David.

Both this national realm and the title Son of David are implied by the pattern of ever-widening concentric circles which describe the sphere of each temptation's effect. The first temptation is in the private realm—the creation of food for oneself. The third temptation is in the international realm—the possession of all the kingdoms of the earth. In conformity to this pattern the second temptation would be expected to be in the national realm. The place of the temptation is significantly upon the pinnacle of the Temple in Jerusalem, the capital city of the nation, thus confirming the national realm of the temptation's impact.

Christ's role as Son of David seems to be stressed by the structure of the account, too. Matthew, in the genealogy of Christ at the beginning of the gospel, stresses Christ's roles as Son of God, Son of David, and Son of Abraham—particularly the latter two. Then in the temptation account, these roles are evidently assumed and stressed again. Working from the broadest concentric circle, the title "Son of Abraham" is paramount in the offer of all the kingdoms of the earth because as son of Abraham, Christ was to bring blessing to all the families of the earth. In other words, both the temptation and the title are in the international realm. In the smallest concentric circle, perhaps the title "Son of God" is most paramount because this is Satan's initial challenge to the proclamation of sonship made at the baptism (although admittedly this is not as clear). In conformity to this pattern, the title "Son of David" is left to be paramount in the second temptation. And this it is, because as "Son of David," He would reign as king over the nation. So both the title and the temptation would be in the national realm. And thus the structure of the account is indeed seen to stress the national realm of the temptation and the title associated with that realm, the "Son of David."

So not only does Christ's potential fulfillment of a Messianic psalm but also the structure of the temptation account itself draw attention to the national Messianic significance of the second temptation.

6. The Greek word *bios* rendered "life" in some translations is likely more accurately rendered "possessions," as the New International Version has done. This is an established usage in the N.T. (Luke 8:43; 15:30), but more importantly it is the sense given the word in John's only other usage of it in 1 John 3:17: "Whoever has the [*bios*—possessions] of this world, and beholds his brother in need and refuses to have compassion upon him, how can the love of God abide in him?"

7. This was not their first test, however. Their lack of

water was the first recorded test (Exod. 15:22-26). But the particular lack of food commented upon by Moses was their first test of several over lack of food. And since it immediately followed the test and consequent lesson over lack of water, it might be considered the first blatant failure of the wilderness testing.

8. Admittedly, there is extensive narrative between the second test in Exodus 17 and the idolatry of Exodus 32. But that very narrative serves merely to highlight this third failure. For those intervening chapters record, for the most part, a detailed description of the ritual for genuine worship of God. The most extensive revelation of true worship in history is incredibly followed by the record of Israel's worship of the golden calf. And in sequence of the nation's recorded failures of tests, it is indeed the third.

9. A more extensive treatment of the particular emphases of Luke may be found in Donald Guthrie's *New Testament Introduction* (Downers Grove, Ill: Inter-Varsity, 1970), pp. 90-93.

10. The "son of" is understood by the genitive *tou theou,* assuming the original *huios* of Luke 3:23.

11. Luke frequently teaches his readers important truths by this invitation to compare two individuals. For example, in the beginning of his gospel, he alternately contrasts the announcement of John's conception (1:5-25) with that of Jesus (1:26-56); then John's birth (1:57-80) with the birth of Jesus (2:1-20). By so comparing the persons, the reader learns right from the start that their activities will be intimately related. Or again, the account of Stephen's death in Luke's Acts of the Apostles is set against the background of Jesus' death in Luke's gospel. In both cases, the last words are requests: (1) to receive the spirit of each (Luke 23:46; Acts 7:59), and (2) to forgive their murderers (Luke 23:34; Acts 7:60). Luke has taught us

implicitly through Stephen that a disciple will follow his master wherever He leads.

One more example of many instances of implicit comparison may be seen in Luke's recording of the conversion of Lydia (Acts 16:11-15) and the conversion of the Philippian jailer (Acts 16:16-34). The first is a quiet conversion where the sovereignty of God is stressed ("The Lord opened her heart"), whereas the second is a dramatic one where human responsibility is stressed ([*You*] "believe on the Lord Jesus"). By placing these conversions side by side, the reader observes: first, the diverse circumstances under which people come to the same Christ, and second, both the human and divine responsibilities which effect conversion.

So it is evident from these few examples that characteristic of Lucan style is the instructive comparison of individuals. In conformity to this style is the implicit comparison of Adam and Christ.

Chapter 4

1. "Flesh and blood" is a phrase used frequently to designate humanity in contrast to God or purely spiritual beings (Gal. 1:16; Eph. 6:12; Heb. 2:14).
2. Cullmann argues cogently for this identification. First, he observes that it is impossible to distinguish in meaning *petros* (the word transliterated "Peter" and meaning "rock") from *petra* (translated "rock"). Both words have the same field of meaning in ordinary usage in Greek.

   Some have tried to draw a distinction between them from the masculine gender of *petros* and the feminine gender of *petra*. However, the masculine gender of *petros* was likely used because it was functioning as a name for a man, whereas the feminine gender of *petra* was the customary gender for the word.

Moreover, Cullmann observes that in the probable Aramaic original of this saying, the morphology of the word would have been identical. "Cepha" would have been used for both Peter and rock. So the original would have read, "Thou art Cepha, and upon the Cepha I will build My church." This observation seems to make even more certain the identification of cepha and cepha—or in Greek, *petros* and *petra*, Peter and the rock.

Oscar Cullmann, *Theological Wordbook of the New Testament*, Vol. 4 (Grand Rapids: Eerdmans, 1968), p. 99.

William Hendriksen, who shares the view of Cullmann, has several noteworthy qualifications to this identification. "Jesus promises to build His church:

a. "Not on Cephas as he was by nature but on him considered as a product of grace. By nature this man was, in a sense, a weakling, very unstable, as has been indicated. . . . By grace he became a most courageous, enthusiastic, and effective witness of the truth the Father had revealed to him with respect to Jesus Christ, the Son of the living God. It was in that sense that Jesus used Peter in *building*—gathering and strengthening—His church.

b. "Not on Cephas considered all by himself, but on Cephas as 'first (Matt. 10:2) among equals,' that is, in 'Peter taking his stand with the eleven' (Acts 2:14). The authority, which in Matthew 16:19 is entrusted to Peter, is, in 18:18, given to the twelve (see also John 20:23). In fact, in the exercise of this authority, the local congregation must not be ignored (Matt. 18:17).

"When the Lord spoke the words recorded here in 16:18-19, He certainly did not mean that Peter could now begin to 'lord it' over the other disciples. The others did not understand it in that way (18:1; 20:20-24), and Jesus definitely rejected any such interpretation (20:25-28; cf. Luke 22:24-30). If Peter himself had conceived of his own authority or that of others as being that of a dictator, how could he have written the beautiful passage in 1 Peter 5:3.

c. "Not on Cephas as the primary foundation. In the primary or basic sense of the term there is only one foundation, and that foundation is not Peter but Jesus Christ Himself (1 Cor. 3:11). But in a secondary sense, it is entirely legitimate to speak of the apostles, including Peter, as the church's foundation, for these men were always pointing away from themselves to Jesus Christ as the one and only Savior. Striking examples of this are found in Acts 3:12 and 4:12. In that secondary sense, Scripture itself refers to the apostles as the church's foundation (Eph. 2:20; Rev. 21:14)." William Hendricksen, *New Testament Commentary, Exposition of the Gospel of Matthew* (Grand Rapids: Baker Book House, 1973), pp. 647-648.

3. The phrase "gates of Hades" likely means "death" or "the place of the dead" when it is used in the Old Testament and apocryphal literature. For example, Hezekiah anticipates death and registers the following complaint, "In the middle of my life I am to enter the *gates* of Sheol [Hades]; I am to be deprived of the rest of my years" (Isa. 38:10, itals. added). So also in The Wisdom of Solomon 16:13; 2 Maccabees 5:51. The phrase "gates of Hades" seems also to be virtually synonymous with the phrase "gates of death" (Psalm 9:13; 107:18).

4. This figure of speech in which the keys represent authority has its precedent in Isaiah 22:22. In this passage, Eliakim was given the keys of the house of David to represent the authority he received in that ruling house.

5. "After a criminal's condemnation he was made to

carry the crossbeam *(patibulum)* to the scene of his torture and death, always outside the city, while a herald carried in front of him the title, the written accusation. It was this *patibulum,* not the whole cross, which Jesus was too weak to carry, and which was borne by Simon the Cyrenian." J. B. Torrance, "Cross," *New Bible Dictionary* (Grand Rapids: Eerdmans, 1962), p. 279.

6. At least seven different interpretations have been given to this statement. It has been suggested that the "coming in His kingdom" which would be seen was: (1) His second advent, (2) His resurrection and ascension, (3) Pentecost, (4) the destruction of Jerusalem, (5) the spread of Christianity, (6) an inner awakening that the kingdom had come, or (7) the transfiguration event (Alfred Plummer, *Luke, I.C.C.* (Edinburgh: T. & T. Clark, 1922), pp. 249-250.

Three lines of argument support the seventh suggestion. First, no interpretation can be accurate which does not explain the reference to "certain ones" of the twelve who would see the event. The phrase indicates that only a few of the twelve would see it. And this one observation leaves only the destruction of Jerusalem and the transfiguration as options because the majority (not the minority) saw the other events. But since the destruction of Jerusalem seems remote to the context, the transfiguration reference is firmly supported by the first line of argument.

Second, the contextual sequence of events supports it. No sooner does Christ make this prediction than we read "and six days later" the transfiguration occurred. Matthew thus draws attention to the fact that the transfiguration itself would have occurred by the way he reckons time (see below) on the seventh day after the prediction. This is a very significant signpost. For Matthew, like others of his background, regarded the number seven as a number of completion and fulness. So in telling us that the transfiguration occurred on the seventh day after the prediction, he has told us symbolically that the event occurs on the day of the prediction's completion and fulfillment. So not only the implication that a minority of the disciples would see the event, but also the contextual sequence of events supports the view that the fulfillment of Christ's prediction comes in the transfiguration.

But third, and most decisively, Peter interprets the transfiguration as just such a fulfillment. And he was present at both the prophetic announcement and the transfiguration. For he entitles what he saw at the transfiguration as "the power and coming of our Lord Jesus Christ" (2 Pet. 1:16-18).

It is not surprising that although the prediction by Christ has indeed been interpreted several ways, the early Fathers of the church and the recent commentaries by Cranfield *(Mark)* and Lane *(Mark)* have understood its fulfillment to be in the transfiguration, too.

7. Luke states that the event was eight days later. As many commentators have noted, this reflects an alternative way of reckoning time in the ancient world. A part of a day could be reckoned as a whole day. And evidently Luke considered it so, but (at least with respect to this event) Matthew did not. Thus, if the prophecy were made on Monday and fulfilled a week from the following Tuesday, then Luke would have counted the part of the Monday and the part of the Tuesday and consequently recorded an eight-day interval. On the other hand, Matthew would have counted only the complete days in between and have recorded a six-day interval with the transfiguration on the seventh day.

8. Compare Matthew 5:17; 7:12; 11:13; 22:40; Luke 16:16;

Acts 24:14 with Luke 16:29, 31; Acts 26:22.

9. George Foot Moore, *Judaism*, Vol. 2 (Cambridge: Harvard University Press, 1954), pp. 357-358.
10. B. L. Smith, "Elijah," *New Bible Dictionary* (Grand Rapids: Eerdmans, 1962), p. 364.
11. 1 Kings 17:8-24; 2 Kings 4:1-37.
12. From "Our Secret Hope," a sermon preached by the Reverend John Trent, April 1976.

Chapter 5

1. In this verse of the psalm is a significant textual problem. Some manuscripts read "pierced through," and others read "like a lion" in its place. Although the external evidence is quite divided, there is enough evidence from the versions, the Massorah, and a few manuscripts of the Hebrew to favor the reading "pierced through." The internal evidence would, of course, favor the verb since the alternative "like a lion" is one which renders no sense to the passage.
2. Frederic W. Farrar, *The Life of Christ* (New York: E. P. Dutton and Company, 1874), p. 440.
3. The paralytic was lame, for example, but Jesus dealt first with his need for forgiveness (Mark 2:1-12). And even when Jesus performed miracles for the provision of food, it was subservient to His purpose of demonstrating that He Himself was the Bread of Life. John, therefore, calls the miraculous creation of bread a sign, that which testifies to another truth.
4. The natural brothers (or more technically, half-brothers) of Jesus are mentioned in the following passages: Matthew 12:46-50; Mark 3:31-35; John 2:12; 7:3-5; Acts 1:14; 1 Corinthians 9:5; Galatians 1:19.
5. S. Lewis Johnson, "The Death of Christ," *Bibliotheca Sacra*, Vol. 125, #497 (Dallas: Dallas Theological Seminary, 1968), p. 14.

Chapter 6

1. Yohanan Aharoni, *The Land of the Bible*, trans. A. F. Rainey (Philadelphia: The Westminster Press, 1967), p. 41.
2. Ibid., p. 41.
3. See appendix, The Unfolding Story of the Scripture.
4. In the opening chapters of John's gospel, it seems transparent that his literary structure revolves around a sequence of four couplets: two public events (2:1-11; 2:13-22); two private conversations (3:1-21; 4:1-26); two conversations with disciples—John the Baptist with his (3:22-36) and Christ with His (4:27-38)—each neatly following one of the two private conversations; and two miracles of healing (4:46-54; 5:1-9). Furthermore, the literary structure is seen to be deliberate because of the obvious comparisons and contrasts within each of the four couplets. In the two public events, one sees (a) grace at a social event in one, and (b) truth at a religious event in the other. In the two conversations, one sees (a) a man at the top of social status seeking Christ by night, and (b) a woman at the bottom of social status sought by Christ at midday. In the two conversations with the disciples, one sees (a) John the Baptist directing his disciples to belief in Christ, not himself, and (b) Christ directing His disciples to growth in Him, not another. In the two miracles, one sees (a) a miracle with Christ not present for a man at the top of social status, and (b) a miracle with Christ present for a man at the bottom of social status.
5. C. S. Lewis, *The Lion, the Witch and the Wardrobe* (New York: Macmillan, 1965), p. 64.
6. Ibid., p. 104.
7. R. H. Charles, *Apocrypha and Pseudepigrapha of the New Testament* Vol. 1, "Wisdom of Solomon," 18:15-18 (London: Oxford University Press, 1913), p. 565.

8. Palestinian Targum on Genesis 49:11.
9. The LXX translator has rendered "rod" by "word" and hence the LXX reads, "He will strike the earth with the *word* of His mouth." John, of course, was familiar with this LXX reference to Christ striking the earth with the word of His mouth. But since he has just quoted a phrase referring to Christ's word as a sword, it is equally as accurate for him to say that Christ strikes the earth with a sword (as he does say in Revelation) as to say He strikes it "with His word" (as the LXX Isa. 11:4 reads) or "with the rod of His mouth" (as the M.T. Isa. 11:4 reads).
10. Once again John has quoted the LXX translation rather than the M.T. The M.T. vowel pointing renders the verb "shatter," whereas the LXX translator imposed a different vowel pointing on the consonants and consequently read the verb as "rule" or "shepherd." In either case the meaning is the same: He rules with force.
11. R. H. Charles, *The Revelation of St. John,* Vol. 2, I.C.C. (Edinburgh: T. & T. Clark, 1920), p. 137.

Chapter 7

1. St. Augustine, *Sermons on the Liturgical Seasons,* trans. Sister Mary Sarah Muldowney, R.S.M., Vol. 38 in *The Fathers of the Church,* ed. Roy Joseph Deferrari (New York: Fathers of the Church, Inc.), p. 28.
2. Blaise Pascal, *Pascal's Pensees* (New York: E. P. Dutton and Co., 1958), pp. 49-50.
3. Ibid., p. 51.
4. Benjamin Breckenridge Warfield, *The Person and Work of Christ,* ed. Samuel Craig (Philadelphia: The Presbyterian and Reformed Publishing Co., 1950), pp. 563-564.
5. Ibid., p. 575.

Appendix

In the very beginning for a brief time, God's ultimate purpose was a reality. In uncluttered simplicity, the Creator governed the earth. The earth was subject to man, and man was subject to God.

When man sinned, however, the harmony was broken. Earth resisted man and would not yield its food without sweat and labor in the midst of thorns. Man resisted man from the pain of birth through the conflicts of life. And man resisted God—fleeing from His presence, straying from His precepts, disregarding His love. And not until Christ returns will all this resistance come to an end. Then the harmony once lost will finally be restored.

And God's intention to do so was clear from the beginning. For God promised from the beginning that the evil one would be defeated (Gen. 3:15). And when this occurred, mankind and earth, under Satan's rule, would return to the God who made them. Precisely how this would happen became more and more clear as time went on. Like a city on a distant horizon, which slowly comes into focus, so God's plans crystallized to regain a people and the earth.

The focus was first sharpened significantly when God promised Abraham that from his descendants would come a nation that would ultimately bless the entire earth (Gen. 12:1-3). The nation was Israel and its blessing to the earth was intended to be foreshadowed through its example and rule. For it was commissioned not only to exemplify God's righteousness, but also to extend His rule over the earth. And through its prophets, priests, and kings, it was designed to fulfill those responsibilities.

The kings were intended to mediate God's rule to man, the priests to mediate for man to God, and the prophets to proclaim God's revelation and guard its practice.

At times, it appeared that blessing through these mediators would come. The rule of the king was just and wise; the worship of the priests was faithful and sincere; the message of the prophets was uncompromising and clear. Nevertheless, for the most part, these mediators and, consequently, the nation fell far short of their responsibilities. The kings often depended on their own strength or that of other nations and served idols rather than God. The priests sometimes worshiped at best in heartless ritual, and at worst in heathen temples. The prophets' message could often be purchased by the highest bidder, and so he spoke for men and not for God.

But God's purpose never changed. He still intended through that nation's Messiah to rule a people and the earth. And the true prophets of God continued to proclaim that message. The nation of Israel would be judged, they said. But her Messiah would reign in a future kingdom not only over Israel but over every nation upon the planet.

And He would do so because He was the great Prophet, the great Priest, and the great King all in one. As the great Prophet, He would not only bring a new revelation, but speak the message of God without compromise. As the great Priest, He would not only pray for His followers but bring them to the Father through His sacrifice. And as the great King, He would not only be entitled to rule the earth in the present but would in actuality rule the earth completely in the future.

So from the very beginning, God intended to counter the work of Satan and regain a people and the earth. And ultimately it was revealed that through the Messiah of Israel this would be done. He would die to gain the people and return to gain the earth.

Moody Press, a ministry of the Moody Bible Institute, is designed for education, evangelization and edification. If we may assist you in knowing more about Christ and the Christian life, please write us without obligation to: Moody Press, % MLM, Chicago, Illinois 60610.